"I have been a disciple-making pastor for over four decades. Twenty years ago I discovered Dr. Anderson's teachings, and they revolutionized my approach to ministry. Life is a spiritual battle—not a Sunday school picnic—and Neil's message is a practical way to win this battle. Neil helped me realize that repentance, faith, forgiveness, and knowing our identity in Christ are essential for making disciples in the local church. Read, study, and learn from this book."

Pastor David Jenkins, Evangelical Free Church

"I have been involved in local church leadership for over thirty years. In that time I have always endeavored to ensure that Christians are discipled rather than treated as merely 'sermon fodder.' Over the years I have tried a number of different approaches to discipleship. Some have been more successful than others. However, I have found the Freedom in Christ approach to be the most consistently effective aid to practical Christian discipleship. I have been using FIC material for over fifteen years now, and it is still proving to be fruitful."

Pastor John Groves, Hope Church Winchester, England

"We have found the Freedom in Christ course to be invaluable for our church community. We introduced FIC two years ago with our pastors and leaders. Since then we've had well over four hundred people go through FIC, with amazing testimonies of healing and freedom impacting people's lives. Freedom in Christ will continue to be a major part of Bayside Church's pathway of discipleship. We highly recommend this book and the Freedom in Christ course."

Rob and Christie Buckingham, senior ministers,
Bayside Church, Melbourne, Australia

"God has gifted Dr. Anderson with the ability to systematize truth in a way that touches the intellect and transforms the heart. I have introduced his teaching in France, Switzerland, and Belgium. The response has been overwhelming, and lives have been revolutionized."

Dr. Walter Stuart, missionary to France; adjunct professor,
Tyndale Theological Seminary, Holland,
and Geneva Bible Institute, Switzerland

D1733353

"We have found the truth that Dr. Anderson teaches and the way in which he presents the message are absolutely vital to effective and sustained discipleship. The message and method of Freedom in Christ Ministries are crucial in helping both new Christians and those who have known Christ longer to walk in freedom in Christ and to make reproducing disciples. That is why we recommend this book to help carry out our Lord's mandate to make disciples of all people."

Dr. Rick and Laurel Langston,
International School of Theology, Singapore

"I first met Dr. Anderson more than twenty years ago when he did a Freedom in Christ conference in the church I was pastoring. Lives were changed when they heard the good news of who they are in Christ and had the opportunity to repent and find their freedom in Christ. Building on his internationally acclaimed Christ-centered teaching, Neil is now bringing to the global church a proven strategy for making fruitful disciples. His teaching on discipleship will change your life, ground you in your position in Christ, and move you forward in the power of Christ. I can't recommend it highly enough."

Dr. Byron Spradlin, president,
Artists in Christian Testimony International

"The message of Freedom in Christ Ministries has touched thousands of lives in South Africa, and it has liberated me as a pastor. Just knowing that I am not responsible *for* others, but responsible *to* others, in terms of ministry, and knowing that I am accepted, secure, and significant in Christ has taken off the pressure of trying to have a 'successful' ministry. All that God desires is that I be a godly minister of the gospel."

Rev. Jonothan Christie, Methodist minister, South Africa

"The evil one has mined the path of 'making disciples of all nations' with lies and deception. Almost as one crying in the wilderness, Dr. Neil Anderson teaches us again that freedom is available to anyone who would read and believe God's Word, place trust in the 'Wonderful Counselor,' and believe what He has to say to the church!"

Dr. David Kyle Foster, president, Mastering Life Ministries

"I have found Dr. Anderson's materials to be an invaluable tool in helping the men we are discipling. *Victory Over the Darkness*, *The Bondage Breaker*, and *Discipleship Counseling* are used on a daily basis. The Steps to Freedom in Christ are critical in helping the men become free from past trauma, unresolved conflicts, and their own misunderstanding of who they are in Christ. Every thought, every idea is supported by Scripture and presented in an easy-to-understand format. Because of God's Word and the resources He has provided through Freedom in Christ Ministries, I personally am a free man in Christ!"

Derek Faulkner, executive director,
Renewed Life Ministries Outreach (RLMO)

"My identity was wrapped up in being a mother and the wife of a pastor. With the children leaving home, I was looking for a greater sense of purpose and thought I would find it by leading the Freedom in Christ course. But to my surprise I learned from the course that my identity is found in Christ and not in what I do. A mild depression left and two people said I appeared happier. So many lives were impacted, and many testified of feeling light, happy, and warm all over."

Lisa Fenton, Hastings, New Zealand

"The Freedom in Christ course connects the truth of God's Word to our everyday reality, allowing for a precious time of discussion on relevant issues. Individuals are given the opportunity to examine themselves and are shown from God's Word how they can overcome the challenges of life."

Majlind Gegprifti, Kisha Rilindja
(The Reborn Church),Tirana, Albania

"For many years Dr. Neil Anderson's books *Victory Over the Darkness* and *The Bondage Breaker* have been a great blessing to the church in India across denominations, and many in our own churches have been impacted. With the Indian church's practice of legalism on one end of the spectrum and the emerging 'hyper-grace' teachings on the other end, balanced biblical teaching of grace and truth is much needed, and Freedom in Christ Ministries discipleship resources meet this critical need."

Pastor and church planter Jeyakaran Emmanuel,
Powerhouse Churches, India

"I was in the ministry for more than fifteen years and a defeated Christian when I was introduced to Dr. Anderson's teaching. When I read *Victory Over the Darkness* and *The Bondage Breaker*, I understood my problems and took time to go through the Steps to Freedom in Christ. It was a new day in my life and ministry. I always carry at least one of Dr. Anderson's books wherever I go, and I use the principles from the books in my teachings. Every pastor and Christian worker who longs for a fruitful ministry should read this book, because it will change their ministries with lasting fruit. I am committed to introducing Neil's writings to as many people as possible."

George Philip, country director, Trans World Radio, India

"I had previously read *Victory Over the Darkness* and *The Bondage Breaker* before I attended Dr. Anderson's Discipleship Counseling conference in Chennai, India. I was personally and richly blessed by the balanced blend of psychological and spiritual truth, along with a healthy acknowledgment of spiritual forces. I was able to relate the teaching to the needs of my people and their various struggles."

Rev. Johh Simeon, senior pastor,
Emmanuel Methodist Church, Chennai, India

"My late husband and I were victims of spiritual abuse when we attended a Dr. Anderson's Resolving Personal and Spiritual Conflicts conference. We were both set free from our bitterness when we forgave that pastor, and I had seventy-five others I needed to forgive, encompassing decades of abuse, victimization, and even rape. My life changed that day, and we started a Freedom in Christ ministry in a new church. That experience has opened doors for me to teach these same principles of forgiveness and identity in Christ to thousands of leaders across the United States and around the world."

Sheryl Giesbrecht, DDiv, author,
Get Back Up: Trusting God When Life Knocks You Down;
radio host and director of public relations, KAXL Life FM;
executive director, International Christian Ministries

"Few ministers have this kind of in-depth knowledge, wisdom, and insight for life application of the Scriptures. There are many good theologians. There are many good psychologists. There are very few disciple makers who are able to combine the principles of sound theology and sound psychology as Dr. Anderson does to help fellow Christians grow in Christ."

Dr. Phyllis Davis and Rev. Carrol Davis,
The Journey Pathways to Healing

"Dr. Neil T. Anderson is one of the most important teachers of the gospel in the postmodern era, a friendly and warm human being, and a wise pastoral counselor. His ministry has brought a powerful renewal to our churches, focusing on our identity in Christ, spiritual freedom, and holistic healing, for the purpose of building up new believers and for the consolidation and restoration of more mature believers. Our church regularly and methodically uses Freedom in Christ materials."

Pastor Darío Silva-Silva, founder,
Casa Sobre la Roca Churches, Colombia, South America

"This material has been an amazing tool for the church in Venezuela. It has relieved my counseling load in a much needed way. We have seen people released from their past due to recognizing their position in Christ. They have stopped blaming others and have allowed the Lord to do His work of healing from the inside, and it is changing their outward behavior."

Pastor Adam Nathanson, Caracas, Venezuela

"After nearly ten years of using Freedom in Christ materials, I learned that this ministry is not simply about setting people free from bondages to sin—it is a discipleship ministry that frees people to become Christlike. Freed people make wonderful disciples of Jesus. Our church became more than a hospital for the wounded. We became a school for developing disciples. Over 1,500 people have gone through the Steps to Freedom in Christ and now worship with all their hearts, pray with power, and disciple others."

Dr. Irv Woolf, director, National Coalition for Purity

"I was blessed by this servant of God who wisely presented principles for ministry in our Christian community of different denominations. His anointed teaching on who we are in Christ, winning the battle for our minds, becoming the person God intended us to be, and knowing how to stand firm against spiritual forces opened our eyes to a complete and integrated message that is so necessary in the spiritual life of every believer. Our congregation continues to see great results using Dr. Anderson's Steps to Freedom in Christ."

Pastor Alberto Benigno, past president,
Council of Baptist Pastors of Córdoba, Argentina

"We are thankful to God for Freedom in Christ Ministries and the blessing it has been to our church. We have employed these materials since we started the church—with excellent results in transformed lives. It is being used constantly in our School of Life in the different levels of classes, resulting in beautiful testimonies. Both *Victory Over the Darkness* and *The Bondage Breaker* are indispensable for discipleship."

Pastor Graciela Sanchez, senior pastor,
New Generation Church, Lanús, Buenos Aires, Argentina

"Freedom in Christ Ministries has had a profound impact on our personal lives and our ministry. As part of an evangelistic ministry for thirty-four years and as a church-growth pastor, we have led many people to Christ. We also had the privilege to lead probably five hundred people through the Steps to Freedom in Christ. Many of those people have expressed that event to be more impacting than their salvation experience. FICM's repentance and discipleship strategy is the key to making fruitful disciples. It has given us the tools to help develop Christians to become the people God desires them to be and to be true followers of Christ."

Earl and Trish Pickard, senior staff,
CRU Ministries

BECOMING A
DISCIPLE-
MAKING
CHURCH
A Proven Method
for Growing **Spiritually
Mature** Christians

NEIL T. ANDERSON

BETHANYHOUSE
a division of Baker Publishing Group
Minneapolis, Minnesota

Published by Bethany House Publishers
11400 Hampshire Avenue South
Bloomington, Minnesota 55438
www.bethanyhouse.com

Bethany House Publishers is a division of
Baker Publishing Group, Grand Rapids, Michigan

Printed in the United States of America

ISBN 978-0-7642-1536-0

Library of Congress Control Number:
2015952319

Chapter 1 adapted from *Victory Over the Darkness*, copyright © 2000, 2013 by Neil T. Anderson. Published by Bethany House. Used by permission.

Chapter 2 adapted from *The Bondage Breaker*, copyright © 1990, 1993, 2000 by Neil T. Anderson. Published by Harvest House Publishers, Eugene, OR 97402, www.harvesthousepublishers.com. Used by permission.

Chapter 3 adapted from *Discipleship Counseling*, copyright © 2003 by Neil T. Anderson. Published by Bethany House. Used by permission.

Chapter 5 adapted from *Getting Anger Under Control*, copyright © 2002 by Neil T. Anderson and Rich Miller. Published by Harvest House Publishers, Eugene, OR 97402, www.harvesthousepublishers.com. Used by permission.

Chapter 6 adapted from *Freedom From Fear*, copyright © 1999 by Neil T. Anderson and Rich Miller. Published by Harvest House Publishers, Eugene, OR 97402, www.harvesthousepublishers.com. Used by permission.

Chapter 7 adapted from *Overcoming Depression*, copyright © 2004 by Neil T. and Joanne Anderson. Published by Bethany House. Used by permission.

Chapter 8 adapted from *Winning the Battle Within*, copyright © 2004, 2008 by Neil T. Anderson. Published by Harvest House Publishers, Eugene, OR 97402, www.harvesthousepublishers.com. Used by permission.

Chapter 9 adapted from *Overcoming Addictive Behavior*, copyright © 2003 by Neil T. Anderson and Mike Quarles. Published by Bethany House. Used by permission.

Chapter 10 adapted from *Setting Your Marriage Free*, copyright © 2006 by Neil T. Anderson and Charles Mylander. Published by Bethany House. Used by permission.

Chapter 11 adapted from *Setting Your Church Free*, copyright © 1995, 2005 by Neil T. Anderson and Charles Mylander. Published by Bethany House. Used by permission.

To protect the privacy of those who have shared their stories with the author, some details have been changed.

Cover design by Rob Williams, InsideOut CreativeArts

16 17 18 19 20 21 22   7 6 5 4 3 2 1

Dedication

We met at the University of Minnesota, where Joanne was working on a home economics degree. We dated briefly, but I left after the first quarter and joined the navy. Five years later I was sitting in a wheelchair at the veterans hospital in Phoenix, Arizona, recovering from knee surgery when she walked through the door. It was love at second sight. Six months later we were married.

Joanne worked as a dietician at St. Luke's Hospital, and then as a home economist for Arizona Public Service while I finished my electrical engineering degree at Arizona State University. We moved back to our beloved Minnesota, where I was employed by Honeywell as an aerospace engineer. We settled into suburban life, and Joanne gave birth to Heidi and Karl. We were the all-American couple living the good life when God called us into ministry.

Joanne typed my papers and manuscripts for two master's theses and two doctoral dissertations until she said, "That is enough," and taught me how to type. But her service to me and the ministry didn't end, because she was the first editor of the seventy-plus books that I typed. Joanne was the most discerning person I know, which was an incredible gift to me given the nature of my ministry. She was a prolific reader, averaging two or three books a week for years, but that stopped about three years ago when her health started to decline. To care for my best friend and partner in life, I suspended all international travel and almost all conference work.

Agitated dementia slowly destroys the brain, and her once-brilliant mind doesn't work very well anymore. She is now in a skilled-nursing/long-term-care facility. I wrote the VICTORY SERIES and this book while visiting her twice a day for the last year and half. Those are the only books that she hasn't edited. The one thing that brightens her day is when I walk through the door. We don't talk much, because it takes too much of her energy. She just wants me there, and I am discovering a deeper purpose in life by fulfilling that need. I am learning the value of simplicity, solitude, and presence. They provide the opportunity to be still and know that He is God. With a heart full of gratitude, I dedicate this book to my beloved wife, Joanne Anderson.

Contents

Introduction

f I only knew then what I know now, my first ten years of ministry would have been radically different. Maybe that is every pastor's story. We all have to start somewhere, and acquiring wisdom and growing in character takes time. Extraordinary gifts and talents can attract a crowd, but no ministry can mature beyond the character of its leaders, or the depth of its message.

My journey began on a farm where I learned the meaning and value of hard work. I attended church every Sunday, and always believed in God, but I didn't come to a saving knowledge of the Lord until many years later. I wasn't ready for college when the time came, so I joined the navy and received electronic technician training. The G.I. Bill helped me get an electrical engineering degree, and I went to work with Honeywell as an aerospace engineer. My wife was a Catholic and I was raised in a Methodist church. We compromised and became Episcopalians. Wrestling was my major sport, but I also pitched for a fast-pitch softball league, played golf in a summer league, and was part of a bowling team. I was the all-American boy who didn't smoke, drink, or sleep around.

I was senior warden (chairman of the board) of an Episcopal church when we were invited to a Lay Institute for Evangelism event. I didn't know what evangelism was. Had I known I probably wouldn't have attended. I was supposed to be learning to share my faith, but I realized I had no relationship with God. It was a humbling experience to discover that I had played church all those years. Everything changed when I gave my heart to Christ. Honeywell transferred me to California, which took me out of my comfort zone. I started a Bible study at work and saw some of my colleagues come to Christ.

Two years later I sensed a call to ministry, but I had no clue what that would entail. I knew very little about myself and God, and I had no idea what my gifts were. A cult could have recruited me at that time. I didn't know one seminary from another, and I am forever grateful that our assistant pastor encouraged me to attend Talbot School of Theology, which was solidly biblical. Who would have guessed that I would be teaching there ten years later?

I had finished four years of engineering school in three years and was not excited about more education, but I loved seminary. It was all new to me. I worked as a club director for Youth for Christ that first year of seminary. Then I was asked to candidate for a half-time position in a large Baptist church as their college pastor. I was only four years old in the Lord, and I knew just a little more than most of the students. After a year I was asked to come on full-time staff and be the college and youth pastor of 250 teenagers. Good things happened, but I knew I wasn't destined to be a youth pastor, and I helped the church recruit someone who was. They invited me to be the minister of adult education, and I started a school of evangelism that resulted in nearly 300 baptisms in one year.

I was flying high when I was asked if I would consider being a candidate for senior pastor at another church. The next four years would appear to be a successful ministry on paper. We started in a rental facility, bought property in a very expensive coastal community, and built new buildings. I was following the party line as best I could, but I started to sense that something was missing. I saw a lot of people come to Christ, but I also saw a lot of wounded people who had problems that I didn't have adequate answers for. I sincerely believed that Christ was the answer and that truth would set people free, but I really didn't know how. I was making converts, but I wasn't making disciples who could reproduce themselves. Additionally, my leadership was being challenged in ways I had never experienced before.

My wife developed cataracts during that pastorate, but they wouldn't do lens implants in those days unless you were over sixty. Joanne was nearly blind when they removed the lens, and later prescribed contact lenses. Being a pastor's wife is a challenge in and of itself, but losing your eyesight made it intolerable for Joanne. I made a commitment to get her out of that role, and that was my motivation to work on my first doctorate. After we moved into our new church facilities and were stabilized as a ministry, I resigned my position and took a year off for study. I was completing my dissertation when I was asked to join the faculty of Talbot School of Theology. That invitation came out of the blue. I had never once considered that as an option. Within two years I was chairman of the practical theology department.

In reality I was going back to seminary as a learner, searching for answers to critical questions that had dogged me for years. The people I had led to Christ were forgiven, but I saw little evidence that they were new creations in Christ. Most, if not nearly all, seemed to have the same old struggles. People that I taught may have become more knowledgeable, but they were not necessarily more mature. Additionally, some were being spiritually oppressed, but I didn't have a clue how to help them.

Having taught evangelism in churches and seminary, I thought I had a good handle on the gospel, but I didn't.

I was searching for answers myself when I offered a master of theology elective, Resolving Personal and Spiritual Conflicts. I had 19 students sign up the first year, 23 the next year, 65 the next year, then 150, and 250. The numbers in the last two years included people off campus who asked to audit the class. Those were very high numbers for a fourth-year elective—fewer than ten students would be closer to the norm. I suffered through a lot of paradigm shifts during that time, but I started to see the lives of my students literally change.

God was sending people to me with every conceivable problem during my tenure at Talbot, and I slowly learned how Christ can heal their wounds and set them free. Just as my ministry was taking off, God took my wife and me through the darkest period of our lives. For fifteen months I didn't know whether Joanne was going to live or die. During that time we lost everything we had financially. We had purchased a house, but had to sell it to pay off Joanne's medical expenses. In the end, God was all we had, and we began to discover that God is all we need. I believe there were two reasons why God took us through that trial. First, I think I was a caring person before, but not to the degree that I am now. Second, God brought me to the end of my resources in order that I may discover His. I had no idea how much my self-sufficient, stoic, left-brained Norwegian background was my greatest enemy to my sufficiency in Christ. Freedom in Christ Ministries was born out of that brokenness. Every book I have written and every recording I have made were all after that experience. I wasn't any smarter. I was just more dependent. That was the birth of Freedom in Christ Ministries.

What I have learned is so transferrable that it is being used all over the world by almost every conservative denomination. I am writing this book having just returned from Freedom in Christ

Ministries' twenty-fifth anniversary international retreat, which included representatives from twenty-seven countries. There were no professional musicians, slick speakers, backslappers or backstabbers, and no prima donnas. Just a group of humble, godly people who love the Lord and each other. We don't own anything. We don't charge for counseling or go where we are not invited, and we raise our own support. Our purpose is to equip the church worldwide, enabling them to establish their people, their marriages, and their churches alive and free in Christ through genuine repentance and faith in God.

In this book I want to share a message and a strategy for how your church can make disciples who can reproduce themselves. I will begin with an overview of the whole discipling process. Consider this book a pastoral briefing on the major ills that befall the church, and how they can be overcome in Christ. I may be the only pastor who has written books on marriage, parenting, anger, depression, anxiety disorders, chemical and sexual addiction, reconciliation, and corporate conflict resolution. I believe the whole world and all its inhabitants are struggling because of the fall, and the only answer is to bring people back into a righteous relationship with God. What I am sharing is a ministry of reconciliation that is accomplished through genuine repentance and faith in God.

A few years ago the Evangelical Free Church asked me to be their speaker at their annual ministry conference. One of their pastors handed me a card with the following note:

> I thank the Lord and you for the materials you have created. God has used you in my life, my marriage, and my ministry. It is so wonderful to use something that works with all sorts of people with all sorts of problems.
>
> I stumbled onto your material a year ago. I used it for Sunday school, and God was using it to prepare us for working with

a severely demonized man. In preparing for helping this man, the elders and I went through the Steps to Freedom in Christ ourselves first. I personally had bondage to sin broken in my life. My wife found freedom from her family's occultic background.

I'm in a new church now. Not much happened the first two months, but without advertising or promoting, God has now sent twelve people to go through the Steps with me. There has been a great work of God in people's hearts. Two elders resigned to get their lives straightened out. One had been having an affair for the last two years. He told me that his hypocrisy didn't bother him until I came. It was the Lord! Not me! I'm honored that God has utilized me to touch lives. I'm taking this elder and his wife through the Steps next week.

I took the other elder and his wife through the Steps last week. He had bondage to pornography, masturbation, and strip joints when he was on business trips. It was wonderful to see both of them find their freedom and renew and deepen their relationship. What a joy and privilege to encourage people as they go through the Steps to Freedom in Christ.

One of our Sunday school teachers was experiencing night terrors and demonic dreams. Through God's "chance events," she told my wife about her difficulties. I took her and her husband through the Steps. When we came to forgiving others, I had to teach, exhort, and encourage her for over an hour. I had to physically put a pencil in her hand. It took another thirty minutes for her to write the first name. Eventually she made a decision and went for it! God is so good! The next Sunday there was so much joy, peace, and freedom on the face of both her and her husband. It is a joy to see people's lives change—to feel the freedom and enjoy their relationship with God.

In an ideal world that pastor shouldn't have graduated from seminary in that condition. Unfortunately, you can graduate from most evangelical seminaries without ever dealing with your own issues. The two elders never should have been considered for such a position, and neither should the Sunday school teacher. I'm thankful the pastor and his wife found the help they needed, and I'm thrilled that they took the initiative to help others. The fact that they had no personal training from us reveals how transferable this message and method is. If I were on the pulpit committee of a church, I would invite him to candidate. Great preachers and gifted musicians can be replaced by a book and a DVD, but a loving pastor who can effectively minister to people in need is harder to find.

His testimony reflects the real world and exposes how inadequately we are trained to disciple others through genuine repentance and faith in God. I'll start by sharing the theological basis for discipleship counseling and a strategy for implementation in your church. The rest of the book will provide the theological basis for overcoming depression, anxiety disorders, anger, chemical and sexual addiction, and marital and church conflicts. This is not a book on theory, or borrowed concepts from the secular world with a few verses sprinkled in. I have seen people all over the world resolve these issues because it is all dependent upon God. I combine discipleship and counseling because I believe a good discipler will also be a good counselor and vice versa. You can't successfully disciple people who are struggling with a multitude of unresolved personal and spiritual conflicts. You don't need a degree in psychology or counseling, because discipleship counseling is an encounter with God, who is the One who grants repentance and sets captives free. But you do need a good grasp of Scripture and a kind, humble spirit.

Dr. Neil T. Anderson

ONE
Victory Over the Darkness

There was a thirty-three-year segment of time when Jesus stepped out of eternity into time in order that we may step out of time into eternity. It began with the incarnation, which was the sternest possible rebuke to human pride. The Word became flesh and dwelt among us. If you and I were to become slugs, it doesn't remotely compare with His humble descent. His physical life ended with the crucifixion, which was the sternest possible rebuke to human selfishness. I will sacrifice my time and energy to help another, and risk my life to save a loved one, but to voluntarily die to save those who are demanding that I be crucified is the ultimate act of selflessness and love. If Jesus just came to set an example, He set the bar far above any realistic human expectations.

That solitary life of Christ is the foundation for making disciples. To understand why, we need to start at the beginning of time. Everything that God created was good. "Then the Lord God formed the man of dust from the ground and breathed into his nostrils the breath of life, and the man became a living creature" (Genesis 2:7 ESV). This unique combination of "dust" and divine breath constituted Adam's original nature and set him apart from the rest of creation. What is often overlooked is that Adam was both physically and spiritually alive. He was physically alive because his soul was in union with his body. He was spiritually alive because his soul was in union with God. "The Lord God commanded the man, saying, 'You may surely eat of every tree of the garden, but of the tree of the knowledge of good and evil you shall not eat, for in the day that you eat of it you shall surely die" (2:16–17 ESV). They ate, and they died. Adam and Eve didn't die physically that day, although that would be a consequence of the fall as well. They died spiritually, because sin had severed their union with God.

They had a divine purpose, which was to rule over the birds of the sky, the beasts of the field, and the fish of the sea. They didn't have to search for significance. They were safe and secure, and they had a deep sense of belonging to God and each other. They were naked and unashamed. They could have sexual intercourse with each other in the presence of God with no sense of guilt and shame. They were safe and secure in His presence. Their attributes have become our glaring needs.

The impact of spiritual death was immediate. Adam tried to hide from God. How does one hide from an omnipresent God? Such a distorted concept of God is a major part of mental illness to this day. Adam was now a natural man who could no longer discern the things of God (see 1 Corinthians 2:14). He was like the Gentiles who walk "in the futility of their mind, being darkened in their understanding, *excluded from the life of God*" (Ephesians 4:17–18, emphasis added). Adam became fearful and anxious. The first emotion expressed by Adam after the fall was "I was afraid" (Genesis 3:10). Anxiety disorders are the number one mental health problem in the world. "Do not fear" is the most repeated commandment in Scripture, occurring around four hundred times. Telling someone to not be afraid, however, doesn't work, because anxiety disorders arise out of a state of disconnection, or disobedience.

Before the fall they were naked and unashamed, but after the fall they wanted to hide and cover up. Their lost innocence was replaced by guilt and shame. Their offspring struggled with depression and anger. Cain brought a grain offering to God, who was not pleased.

> Cain became very angry and his countenance fell. Then the Lord said to Cain, "Why are you angry, and why has your countenance fallen? If you do well, will not your countenance be lifted up? And if you do not do well, sin is crouching at the door; and its desire is for you, but you must master it."
>
> Genesis 4:5–7

Depression is the number two mental health problem in our present world, which is experiencing a blues epidemic in an age of anxiety and getting progressively worse.

What was the cause of their mental and emotional depravity and sinful behavior? There was no pollution of any kind in their environment, and they couldn't blame Mom and Dad. Only one thing changed in their experience. They died spiritually! They were separated from God. If you believe that, then there is only one overarching answer for the mental and emotional problems that plague the world and the church today.

After the fall, every descendent of Adam was born physically alive but spiritually dead. Jesus said, "Truly, truly, I say to you, unless one is born again he cannot see the kingdom of God" (John 3:3). That would seem to be all that is needed, but the fall had another disastrous result. Paul explains, "And you were dead in the trespasses and sin in which you once walked, following the course of this world, following the prince of the power of the air, the spirit that is now at work in the sons of disobedience"

(Ephesians 2:1–2 ESV). Adam and Eve had lost their dominion, and Satan became the rebel holder of authority. Jesus referred to Satan as the "ruler of this world" (John 12:31; 16:11). Paul calls him the "prince of the power of the air" and "the god of this world" (2 Corinthians 4:4), and instructed believers to put on the armor of God, "For we do not wrestle against flesh and blood, but against rulers, against the authorities, against the cosmic powers over this present darkness, against spiritual forces of evil in the heavenly places" (Ephesians 6:12 ESV). Concerning our times Paul wrote, "The Spirit clearly says that in later times some will abandon the faith and follow deceiving spirits and things taught by demons" (1 Timothy 4:1 NIV1984). I have found that to be happening right now all over the world. John wrote, "The whole world lies in the power of the evil one" (1 John 5:19).

What a mess! God raised up Moses to deliver the Israelites from Egypt and give them the law, but they couldn't keep it. God sent prophets to correct the people, but they were stoned or largely ignored. The wise, rich, and politically powerful Solomon tried to find purpose and meaning in life independently of God and concluded, "Vanity of vanities! All is vanity" (Ecclesiastes 1:2). Who has the answers for the woes of fallen humanity? I believe the church does.

Then Came Jesus

The most impacting book of my life, other than the Bible, was *The Training of the Twelve* by A. B. Bruce. He wrote, "Jesus was inaugurating a process of spiritual emancipation which was to issue in the complete deliverance of the apostles, and through them of the Christian church."[1] It was the primary text I used when I taught discipleship at Talbot School of Theology, along with *The Master Plan of Evangelism* by Robert Coleman, which was more about discipleship than evangelism. I still recommend those two books above any others for understanding the Master's plan for making disciples.

After four hundred years of silence, the Word became flesh and dwelt among us. "In Him was life, and the life was the light of men" (John 1:4 ESV). All the illumination in the world cannot impart life. What Adam and Eve lost in the fall was life, and that is what Jesus came to give us. Like the first Adam, Jesus was both physically and spiritually alive. His entire life was an example for us to follow. Being fully God and fully man, He had to develop as a man, so He "kept increasing in wisdom [mental] and stature [physical], and in favor with God [spiritual] and men [social]" (Luke 2:52). He submitted to public baptism and was tempted in every way, yet He did not sin. He was thoroughly vetted before He began His public ministry. Since all temptation is an attempt to entice us to live independently of God, Jesus demonstrated total reliance upon the Father, and by doing so He showed us how a spiritually alive person can live a righteous life. He said, "I can do nothing on My own initiative" (John 5:30). "Now they know that everything You have given Me comes from You" (John 17:7).

Jesus said, "The words that I say to you are not just My own. Rather, it is the Father, living in Me, who is doing His work" (John 14:10). Now it is Christ living in us doing His work, which is the essential prerequisite for making disciples. He taught that apart from Christ we can do nothing (John 15:5). Discipleship is not you and I building our natural lives into each other. It is helping each other to become firmly rooted *in Christ* so that we may grow *in Christ* (see Colossians 2:7). This requires some degree of brokenness, because we began our natural life self-centered and self-confident, relying on our own strength and resources.

The Key to Effective Ministry

Jesus didn't confront the disciples right away with that truth, but instead invited them to follow Him. He demonstrated His authority over nature, illnesses, and demons. When He thought they were ready, "He called the twelve together, and gave them power and authority over all the demons and to heal diseases. And He sent them out to proclaim the kingdom of God and to perform healing" (Luke 9:1–2). They could not take anything with them on their journey because He wanted them to be totally dependent upon Him. "When the apostles returned, they gave an account to Him of all that they had done" (Luke 9:10). That sounds like an annual report of a church going nowhere: Look at all the things we did this year! But what did God do? Did they produce any fruit that comes from abiding in Christ? Even though they had authority and power over demons, they were ineffective (see Luke 9:37–41).

A crowd gathered, and the Lord spoke to them about the kingdom of God. But they were in a desolate place, and the twelve told Jesus to send them home for food and lodging. Jesus said, "You give them something to eat" (Luke 9:13). *Us? We only have five loaves and two fish!* It is human nature to think only of our resources when God gives us a seemingly impossible task. So the Lord told them to gather the crowd into groups of fifty, which they did. So give them credit for being obedient. The Lord took what they had and blessed it, and the disciples distributed so much food that all ate and were satisfied. The broken pieces that were left over filled twelve baskets. What an object lesson, but did they get it?

After feeding five thousand people, Jesus told the disciples to get in a boat and row to the other side of the sea. Jesus went up a mountain to pray. In the middle of the night, they were straining at the oars because the wind was against them. Jesus "came to them, walking on the sea; and He intended to pass by them" (Mark 6:48). Jesus intends to pass by the self-sufficient. If you want to row in your own strength against the storms of life, go ahead. Jesus will let you until your arms fall off. But those who call upon the Lord will be saved. When the disciples saw Jesus, they were terrified, thinking it was a ghost. When Jesus got in the boat, "the wind stopped; and they were utterly astonished, for they had not gained any insight from the incident of the loaves, but their heart was hardened" (Mark 6:51–52). How could they miss such an object lesson? I would suspect it was for the same reason we miss them today.

Jesus used this instance to share the central theme of all four gospels—the core message for making reproducible disciples:

> "If anyone wishes to come after Me, he must deny himself, and take up his cross daily and follow Me. For whoever wishes to save his life will lose it, but whoever loses his life for My sake, he is the one who will save it. For what is a man profited if he gains the whole world, and loses or forfeits himself?"
>
> Luke 9:23–25

Those who seek to find their identity and purpose and the meaning of life in their natural existence will lose it. Denying oneself is denying self-rule. We call Him Lord and pray earnestly for His guidance, but we struggle to give up our self-sufficiency. We started our natural existence by saying "I can do it" when we were two years old, and we want to believe that we can. Pride will prevent us from admitting that we can't or that we're wrong. We struggle to hang on to the last vestige of our natural life, while God is orchestrating just the opposite. "For we who live are constantly being delivered over to death for Jesus' sake, so that the life of Jesus also may be manifested in our mortal flesh" (2 Corinthians 4:11).

A missionary doctor provided medical service in a third-world country for two years but never saw one convert, which he believed to be his primary mission. He and his wife were committed to being a positive witness for the Lord, and they did so by living an exemplary life. Then a tragedy struck and their two-year-old son died in a freak accident. The loss of his child and the frustration of seeing no one come to Christ were overwhelming for the young doctor. To safeguard his witness, he ran into the jungle and poured out his anguish toward God. Unbeknownst to him, a native had followed him into the jungle and witnessed his emotional catharsis. He ran back into the village shouting, "White man just like us!" Within months the entire village was Christian.

It seems so sacrificial, but is it really? You are sacrificing the temporal to gain the eternal. You are sacrificing the pleasures of things to gain the pleasures of life. "Godliness is profitable for all things, since it holds promise for the present life and also the life to come" (1 Timothy 4:8). The twelve disciples still had some other hard lessons to learn. The Lord had to confront their unbelief (see Luke 9:37–45), pride (vv. 46–48), possessiveness (vv. 49–50), erroneous spirit (vv. 51–56), false confidence (vv. 57–58), and lame excuses (vv. 59–62). Be prepared for boot camp when you sign up for the Lord's service. Those who come to the end of themselves have transformational ministries; those who don't simply share information and coordinate programs. We can't impart to others what we don't possess ourselves.

Kingdoms in Conflict

The Lord appointed seventy others and sent them out, but they came back with a different report than the twelve did. "The seventy returned with joy, saying, 'Lord, even the demons are subject to us in Your name'" (Luke 10:17). Jesus said, "Behold,

I have given you authority to tread on serpents and scorpions, and over all the power of the enemy, and nothing will injure you. Nevertheless do not rejoice in this, that the spirits are subject to you, but rejoice that your names are recorded in heaven" (vv. 19–20). That is an important attitude check for servant leaders. Don't rejoice that you have authority over others, but rejoice that you are a child of God. The last thing the devil wants you to know is who you are in Christ. Jesus also implies that we should focus on the answer, not the problem. All the analysis in the world doesn't set anyone free.

Discipleship is kingdom building, and the opposition is the kingdom of darkness. The Bible portrays a battle between those two kingdoms, which is a battle between good and evil, between true prophets and false prophets, between the Spirit of truth and the father of lies, and between the Christ and the anti-Christ. Adam and Eve forfeited their right to rule, and Satan became the rebel holder of authority. After the resurrection Jesus said, "All authority has been given to Me in heaven and on earth. Go therefore and make disciples of all the nations, baptizing them in the name of the Father and the Son and the Holy Spirit" (Matthew 28:18–19). Who has the right to rule is *the* question when there are two kingdoms in conflict.

Jesus never appealed to His authority as the basis for what He did and spoke, yet "He was teaching them as one having authority, and not as their scribes" (Matthew 7:29). He did, however, reference His authority in giving the Great Commission, because one cannot delegate responsibility without authority. Authority and power were initially given only to the twelve and the seventy, but that would change after Pentecost. The disciples were told to wait in Jerusalem until they received power—when the Holy Spirit would come upon them (see Acts 1:8). Only then could they be effective witnesses, because the resurrected life of Christ would be within them.

Pentecost was the beginning of the church, and now every born-again believer has the authority and power to do God's will. Power is the ability to rule, and authority is the right to rule; every true believer who is dependent upon God has both, because of who we are in Christ. Those who seek to build their own kingdom in the flesh have neither the power nor the authority. Our ability to make disciples is all based on our identity and position in Christ, which the apostle Paul explains in Ephesians 1:1–2:10.

He starts by explaining our inheritance in Christ and prays . . .

> that the eyes of your heart may be enlightened, so that you will know what is the hope of His calling, what are the riches of the glory of His inheritance in the saints, and what is the surpassing greatness of His power toward us who believe. These are in accordance with the working of the strength of His might which He brought about in Christ, when He raised Him from the dead and seated Him at His right hand in the heavenly places, far above all rule and authority and power and dominion.
>
> Ephesians 1:18–21

We are also seated with Christ in the heavenlies (see 2:6), which is the spiritual realm. It is His power and His authority, which we share because of our position in Christ and when we are filled with His Spirit. Therefore, "be strong in the Lord and in the strength of His might" (Ephesians 6:10).

I have had the privilege of helping believers resolve their personal and spiritual conflicts and find their freedom in Christ all over the world, and I have observed one common denominator for every defeated Christian. None of them knew who they are in Christ, nor did they understand what it meant to be a child of God. John wrote, "But as many as received Him, to them He gave the right to become children of God" (John 1:12). If the "[Holy] Spirit Himself testifies with our spirit that we are children of God, and if children, heirs also, heirs of God and fellow heirs with Christ" (Romans 8:16–17), why weren't they sensing that? Why are so many believers ignorant of their spiritual inheritance?

Where Is the Repentance?

In my travels around the world, I have observed two glaring deficiencies. The first is the lack of genuine repentance. Jesus said, "The time is fulfilled, and the kingdom of God is at hand; repent and believe in the gospel" (Mark 1:15). Paul said, "Being then the children of God, we ought not to think that the Divine Nature is like gold or silver or stone, an image formed by art and thought of man. Therefore having overlooked the times of ignorance, God is now declaring to men that all people everywhere should repent" (Acts 17:29–30). John the Baptist preached repentance, and when the Pharisees came to be baptized, he said to them, "You brood of vipers, who warned you to flee from the wrath to come? Therefore bear fruit in keeping with repentance" (Matthew 3:7–8). Paul "kept declaring to those of Damascus first, and also Jerusalem and then throughout all the region of Judea, and even to the Gentiles, that they should repent and turn to God, performing deeds appropriate to repentance" (Acts 26:20). Where is the fruit in keeping with our repentance?

People all over the world come to churches carrying a lot of baggage. They hear a good message, sing some songs, and pick up their baggage and take it back home with them. There are many opportunities for Christians to be educated in their faith, but very few opportunities exist to repent, and in most cases we are not sure how. I didn't know how to help people resolve their mental, emotional, and spiritual conflicts when I was a pastor. Most believers understand confession, but if that is all they are doing, they are trapped in the sin, confess, sin, confess, and sin again cycle. Do we really believe that repentance and faith in God is the only effective and lasting means by which we can resolve personal and spiritual conflicts? If that is a new concept for you, please give me a chance to explain what I have learned about conflict resolution based solely on the Word of God.

The Whole Gospel

Second, most believers are laboring under a third of the gospel. They believe that Jesus is the Messiah who came to die for their sins, and hopefully heaven awaits them when they die if they put their trust in God. That is partially true, but that would leave them with the belief that eternal life is something they get when they die, which is not true. "And the testimony is this, that God has given us eternal life, and this life is in His Son. He who has the Son has the life; he who does not have the Son of God does not have the life" (1 John 5:11–12). Let me put it stronger. Hell awaits us if our soul is not in union with God before we physically die. "Test yourselves to see if you are in the faith; examine yourselves! Or do you not recognize this about yourselves, that Jesus Christ is in you—unless indeed you fail the test?" (2 Corinthians 13:5).

The early church defined salvation as union with God. Union with God is most often communicated in the epistles as being "in Christ" or "in Him." There are forty such prepositional phrases in the book of Ephesians alone. Paul said, "Therefore I exhort you, be imitators of me. For this reason I have sent to you Timothy, who is my beloved and faithful child in the Lord, and he will remind you of my ways which are in Christ, just as I teach everywhere in every church" (1 Corinthians 4:16–17). I must be an imitator of Paul, because that is what I do.

What Adam and Eve lost in the fall was life, and that is what Jesus came to give us (see John 10:10). He also came to destroy the works of the devil (see 1 John 3:8), and that final third of the gospel is what most of the world inhabitants are waiting to hear. Spiritism is the most practiced religion of the world. They make offerings to appease the deities, and they consult with shamans, avatars, psychics, witch doctors, and quake doctors to seek guidance and healing. Such occult practitioners seek to manipulate the spiritual world through incantations, curses, etc. We have the privilege to announce that those demonic entities have been disarmed and that believers have authority and power over them. That is the gospel they are waiting to hear, and it is just as much a part of the gospel as is our forgiveness and new life in Christ. Paul summarizes the whole gospel in Colossians 2:13–15:

> When you were dead in your transgressions and the uncircumcision of your flesh, He made you alive together with Him, having forgiven us all our transgressions, having canceled out the certificate of debt consisting of decrees against us, which was hostile to us; and He had taken it out of the way, having nailed it to the cross. When He disarmed the rulers and authorities, He made a public display of them, having triumphed over them through Him.

There are many believers who don't fully understand the whole gospel, which I didn't. I had been in ministry for ten years when the truth of who I am in Christ fully sank in. It was like scales fell from my eyes. Watchman Nee and Hudson Taylor wrote about their experiences of discovering their identity and position in Christ. They cried tears of joy when they realized that they were already alive in Christ and didn't need to strive anymore to become someone they already were. This is not a second work of grace. Being alive and free in Christ is the birthright of every child of God. Do we grow into such an awareness, which seemed to be my experience, or did God intend this truth to be foundational? Scripture would argue for the latter.

The truth can't set you free if you don't know it, which is part of the problem. Lack of repentance is the bigger issue. I can quote Galatians 2:20 to a hurting soul, and the impact is usually zero. But when I help them resolve their personal and spiritual conflicts, the Scriptures come alive. Many have said, "How come I couldn't see this before? Everywhere I read now I see that I'm *in Christ*!"

A pastor with twenty-two years of ministry under his belt came to see me. He said, "I have been struggling for years in ministry, and I think I finally see some glimmer of hope. I was reading Colossians 3:3, 'For you have died and your life is hidden with Christ in God.' That's the key, isn't it?" I assured him that it was, and then He asked me, "How do we do that?" "Have died" is past tense. This dear pastor has been trying to become somebody he already is. I was doing a conference for pastors in England. After two days a sixty-year-old pastor said, "I have been doing prayer seminars around the country based on the Lord's Prayer. This is the first time I have realized that when I said 'Our Father,' I was indeed His child."

A pastor wrote me a letter thanking me for my first two books, *Victory Over the Darkness* and *The Bondage Breaker*. He was the founding pastor of a church that split after sixteen years. It precipitated a tremendous time of learning and growth for him. He said that *Victory Over the Darkness* was especially helpful because he had tried to find too much of his identity in what he did as a pastor and not enough in who he is in Christ.

John Stott wrote:

In practice we should constantly be reminding ourselves who we are. We need to talk to ourselves, and ask ourselves questions: "Don't you know? Don't you know that you have been united to Christ in His death and resurrection? Don't you know that you have been enslaved to God and have committed yourself to His obedience? Don't you know these things? Don't you know who you are?" We must go on pressing ourselves with such questions until we reply: "Yes, I do know who I am, a new person in Christ, and by the grace of God I shall live accordingly."[2]

I have given the following list by way of a bookmark to thousands of struggling Christians. Some read it in disbelief, while most receive it with great joy and relief. One person said, "I didn't know God loved me that much." One inquirer became mentally confused and said the letters of the words were running off the page. She found her freedom.

IN CHRIST

I am accepted:

John 1:12	I am God's child.
John 15:15	I am Jesus' friend.
Romans 5:1	I have been accepted (justified) by God.
1 Corinthians 6:17	I am united with the Lord and one with Him in spirit.
1 Corinthians 6:20	I have been bought with a price—I belong to God.
1 Corinthians 12:27	I am a member of Christ's body, part of His family.
Ephesians 1:1	I am a saint.
Ephesians 1:5	I have been adopted as God's child.
Ephesians 2:18	I have direct access to God through the Holy Spirit.
Colossians 1:14	I have been bought back (redeemed) and forgiven of all my sins.
Colossians 2:10	I am complete in Christ.

I am secure:

Romans 8:1–2	I am free from punishment (condemnation).
Romans 8:28	I am assured that all things work together for good.
Romans 8:31–34	I am free from any condemning charges against me.
Romans 8:35–39	I cannot be separated from the love of God.

2 Corinthians 1:21–22	I have been established, anointed, and sealed by God.
Philippians 1:6	I am sure that the good work that God has begun in me will be finished.
Philippians 3:20	I am a citizen of heaven.
Colossians 3:3	I have died, and my life is hidden with Christ in God.
2 Timothy 1:7	I have not been given a spirit of fear, but of power, love, and a sound mind.
Hebrews 4:16	I can find grace and mercy in time of need.
1 John 5:18	I am born of God, and the evil one cannot touch me.

I am significant:

Matthew 5:13–14	I am the salt of the earth and light of the world.
John 15:1, 5	I am a part of the true vine, joined to Christ and able to produce much fruit.
John 15:16	I have been chosen by Jesus to bear fruit.
Acts 1:8	I am a personal witness of Christ.
1 Corinthians 3:16	I am a temple of God.
2 Corinthians 5:17–21	I am at peace with God and a minister of reconciliation.
2 Corinthians 6:1	I am God's co-worker.
Ephesians 2:6	I am seated with Christ in the heavenlies.
Ephesians 2:10	I am God's workmanship.
Ephesians 3:12	I may approach God with freedom and confidence.
Philippians 4:13	I can do all things through Christ who strengthens me.

36

TWO
Battle for the Mind

H e was known by faculty and students alike as "Mister Personality." He was a gifted communicator with an excellent grade-point average. He possessed all the skills for being a fine pastor, and everyone predicted that he would have a successful ministry. He received a call to be a senior pastor . . . and bombed out in two years. He attended my Living Free in Christ conference and wrote me the following letter:

> I've always figured I was a rotten, no good, dirty, stinking sinner, saved by grace, yet failing God miserably every day. All I could look forward to was a lifetime of apologizing every night for not being the man I know He wants me to be: "But I will try harder tomorrow, Lord." As a firstborn, trying so hard to earn the approval of high-expectation parents, I've related to God the same way. He just couldn't possibly love me as much as He does other, "better" believers. Oh sure, I'm saved by grace through faith, but really I'm just hanging on until He gets tired of putting up with me here, and brings me home to finally stop the failure in progress. Whew! What a treadmill!

Neil, when you said, "You are not a sinner; you are a saint who sins," in reference to our new primary identification, you totally blew me away! Isn't that strange that a man could graduate from a good seminary and never latch on to the truth he is indeed a new creation in Christ? I'm convinced that old tapes laid down in early childhood can truly hinder our progress in understanding who we are in Christ.

Thank you for your clear teaching in this area, which has been liberating for me. I'm beginning to grow out of my old ways of thinking about myself, and about God. I don't constantly picture Him as disappointed in me anymore. If He can still love me and be active in me and find use for me even after I failed Him as badly as I did, then surely my worth to Him can't be based on my performance. He just plain loves me—period. What a new joyful walk I'm experiencing with Him.

I have been so deeply touched by these insights. I am taking our people through a study in Ephesians, learning who we are in Christ and what we as believers have in Christ. My preaching is different, and our people are profiting greatly. Each day of service is a direct gift from God, and I bank each one carefully in heaven's vault for all eternity.

God "rescued us from the domain of darkness, and transferred us to the kingdom of His beloved Son" (Colossians 1:13). We are no longer "in Adam" or "in the flesh"; we are spiritually alive "in Christ" (see Romans 8:9). "Therefore if anyone is in Christ, he is a new creature; the old things passed away; behold, new things have come" (2 Corinthians 5:17). If that is all true, then how come most believers still feel the same way they always had, like the above pastor, and why do they continue to struggle with the same old issues? That is a fair question and one that members of every church should be able to answer.

When we were born dead in our trespasses and sin, we had neither the presence of God in our lives nor the knowledge of

His ways. Consequently, we learned to live independently of God. Then one day we came to Christ, but nobody pushed the Clear button. Everything we learned before Christ is still in our memory bank. That is why Paul wrote, "Do not conform any longer to the pattern of this world, but be transformed by the renewing of your mind" (Romans 12:2). Even as believers, we can continue conforming to the patterns of this world.

Paul describes the psychological and spiritual nature of renewing our minds as a battle:

> For though we live in the world, we do not wage war as the world does. The weapons we fight with are not the weapons of the world. On the contrary, they have divine power to demolish strongholds. We demolish arguments and every pretension that sets itself up against the knowledge of God, and we take captive every thought to make it obedient to Christ.
>
> 2 Corinthians 10:3–5

In the papyri the word *stronghold* or *fortress* also had the meaning of "prison." What are those strongholds, and how are they raised up against the knowledge of God?

Everything we learned before we came to Christ was assimilated from the environment in which we were raised in two primary ways. First, we developed our worldview from prevailing experiences. By that I mean the home we were raised in, the friends and relatives we had, the schools we attended, and the church we did or didn't go to. It is important to note that two children raised in the same home can, and usually will, respond differently to the same environment due to their personal choices and the uniqueness of their God-given gifts, talents, and potentialities. One boy can be raised in a supportive Christian home and believe this world is pretty good. Another boy doesn't know who his birth father is. His mother has multiple sex partners, and some physically abuse him. What is his perception of this world and of himself? Which of those two boys needs Christ the most? Both exactly the same, and we must never forget that, but they are going to struggle with different issues.

Second, our worldview is shaped by traumatic experiences such as physical and verbal abuse, death of a loved one, the divorce of parents, etc. It took me years to realize that people are not in bondage to past traumas; they are in bondage to lies they believe because of the trauma, such as, *I'm no good. God doesn't love me. I'll never measure up. I can't trust anybody.* Essentially, we become prisoners to the lies we believe. These strongholds are mental habit patterns of thought burned into our minds over time, or deeply embedded in our memories due to past traumas. If you suffered harm for telling the truth, you probably learned to lie or blame others. If people are put down for being emotionally honest, they will likely become emotionally insolated and find it difficult to express themselves. Psychologists call such responses defense mechanisms, and we all have them. Theologians would likely call them flesh patterns, which is a larger category that includes defense mechanisms. Flesh patterns represent all learning that is derived independently from God.

Some flesh patterns may appear to be good. Secular counselors operating in the flesh try to help their clients root out defense mechanisms. Secular recovery programs try to help alcoholics achieve sobriety. It is not my nature to be critical of such attempts, but according to Paul, they have built their foundations on wood, hay, and straw, and they will not survive the test of fire (see 1 Corinthians 3:10–15). I don't look down my nose at human efforts to reduce suffering for the relatively short time we have in this temporal world, but I'm saddened that they are not given an eternal solution. My major flesh pattern was self-sufficiency, which I thought was good, but it was my greatest enemy to my sufficiency in Christ. In hindsight I realized that I ran many programs and preached many messages in the flesh. Someone once said that if the Holy Spirit was removed from the church, 95 percent of all the "good" church programs would continue on as scheduled. Since we learned to live separately from God, how then should we live in union with Him?

Toward a Christian Psychology

Believers are part material and part immaterial, described by Paul as an inner person and an outer person (see 2 Corinthians 4:16). Of course, the two work in unison, and the obvious correlation is between the brain and the mind. The brain is part of our physical body and will return to dust when we physically die. When that happens, we will be present with God, but we won't be there mindless, because the mind is part of the soul, as shown here:

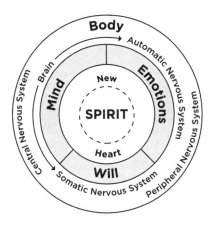

The brain-mind correlation is similar to a computer operation that has two very distinct components, namely the hardware and the software. The hardware is the primary focus of the medical profession when seeking to treat mental and emotional problems. Taking a pill to cure your body is commendable, but taking a pill to cure your soul is deplorable.* If you only consulted your Bible, you would come to the conclusion that the software is the primary issue.

Of course, we can have hardware problems like organic brain syndrome, dementia, and chemical imbalances. The software will struggle to work if the computer is malfunctioning. It is pretty hard to think clearly, much less pray, while suffering a migraine headache. The brain and the spinal cord make up the central nervous system. Stemming from that is a peripheral nervous system, which has two distinct channels. The somatic nervous system is what regulates all our muscular and skeletal movements. It is that part of our body that we have volitional control over. It obviously correlates with our will.

The autonomic nervous system regulates all our glands, which we don't have direct volitional control over. I believe that correlates with our emotions, which we also don't have direct volitional control over. If you think you do, try liking a person who disgusts you. You can't just decide to change your feelings toward that person, but you can choose to love him or her, which is a measure of your character and will. The love (*agape*) of God is not dependent upon the object. God loves us because God is love, which is why His love is unconditional, and that should become increasingly true for us as we become more like Him. What we do have control over is what we think and what we choose to believe.

Spiritual Synergy

To understand how it all fits together, let's consider the problem of stress. God has created us to be able to withstand a

---

* I will discuss brain chemistry and the proper use of medication more in chapter 7, "Overcoming Depression." I believe depression is a malady that must be treated holistically, because it is a body, soul, and spirit problem.

certain amount of stress. When the pressures of life befall us, our adrenal glands respond by excreting cortisol-like hormones into our bloodstreams. That adrenaline rush enables a flight or fight response. If pressures are overwhelming or persist too long, then stress becomes distress, our systems break down, and we become physically sick. But why is it that two people can be subjected to the same degree of stress and one rises to the challenge while the other falls apart? Is it because one has superior adrenal glands? There will be some physical differences between the two, but the primary difference is how they mentally process life events.

To illustrate, consider the Philistines and the Israelites, who were about to head into battle when the Philistines offered a winner-take-all challenge between their champion and anyone the Israelites put forward. The adrenal glands of the Israelites were pumping away, and nobody wanted to step forward. Then along came David, who said, "Who is this uncircumcised Philistine, that he should taunt the armies of the living God?" (1 Samuel 17:26 NASB). Both David and the Israelites had the same data to work with, but they interpreted it differently. David saw Goliath in relation to God, and the others saw Goliath in relation to themselves. Such acts of faith don't happen in a vacuum. The context reveals that David had already seen God deliver him from a lion and a bear.

Let's put it together. The Israelites saw the giant and heard his boasting through their natural senses, and that information was sent to the brain. But it was the mind that evaluated the data, and that is what determined the signal sent to the adrenal glands. The brain cannot function any other way than how it is programmed. People are not affected by their environment; they are affected by how they perceive or what they believe about what is happening around them. Saying to someone, "You shouldn't feel that way," should be stricken from our vocabulary, because people can't volitionally change how they feel. It is a subtle form of rejection. It is more appropriate to say, "I'm not sure you are in possession of all the facts, because you would probably feel differently if you did."

The common tendency is to think that certain activating events are what caused us to feel a certain way: "You made me mad" or "That really ticked me off." Between any activating event and the resultant emotional response is our mental evaluation. Generally speaking, our emotions are a product of our thought life. If what we believe does not conform to truth, then what we feel does not conform to reality. Let me illustrate.

Suppose someone has worked for a company for thirty years and plans to stay in their employment until he retires. The company, however, is downsizing, and he has seen some people laid off. He goes to work Monday morning and finds a note on his desk from his boss. It says, "I need to see you this coming Friday at 10:30 a.m. in my office. Please set that time aside." Can you imagine what would go through his mind that week?

The mind does not deal well with unknowns, and it characteristically makes assumptions to fill in where facts are missing. Human nature usually assumes the worst. Initially, he may think that he is going to be laid off, and the resultant emotional reaction will likely be anger. Then other options come to mind and maybe he isn't going to be laid off. *Well, maybe I am. Then again maybe not, but I probably am.* Now he feels anxious, because he is double-minded, and a double-minded person is unstable in all their ways (see James 1:8). By Thursday he has resigned to the "fact" that he is going to get laid off, and now he is depressed because he feels helpless and hopeless. Reaction to losses is the primary cause for depression, and it doesn't even have to be a real loss. Major depressions can spring from imagined or threatened losses.

44

By Friday morning the poor man is an emotional basket case. In four days he has experienced anger, anxiety, and depression all because of the way he thought. As he enters his boss's office, several other employees are there to congratulate him for being promoted to vice president. Now his feelings suddenly conform to reality, because what he now believes is true. Such reasoning is the basis for cognitive behavior therapy (CBT), which is the most entrenched methodology of both secular and Christian counselors. The basic theory is that people are feeling what they are feeling and doing what they are doing because of what they have chosen to think or believe. Therefore, if you want to change people's behavior and emotional states, you should seek to change what they think and what they consciously choose to believe.

From a truly Christian perspective, that is repentance, which literally means a change of mind. I generally agree with the basic premise of CBT; however, I will explain in the coming chapters why secular and secularized Christian practices of CBT are inadequate. One glaring omission is the reality of the spiritual world, which I will briefly address later in this chapter.

In a general sense, believers possess two plans in their mind. Plan B is the way they learned to live their lives independently of God—i.e., their flesh patterns. Believers also possess plan A, which is God's way, because they have the mind of Christ (see 1 Corinthians 2:16) and the presence of the Holy Spirit, who will lead them into all truth. Every believer has a choice. We can choose to walk after the flesh, or we can walk after the Spirit (see Galatians 5:16–23). Our choices become evident in either the deeds of the flesh or the fruit of the Spirit. The goal is to be transformed by the renewing of the mind and to learn to walk by faith in the power of the Spirit and not carry out the desires of the flesh (see v. 16).

Consider God's plan A for marriage, which is a lifetime monogamous relationship between one man and one woman until the covenant is broken by the death of either spouse. Premarital counseling should make that clear, but the couple should also be encouraged not to entertain thoughts contrary to that commitment, because that is where the battle is won or lost. The temptation may begin with the thought, *I wonder what it would be like to be married to him or her?* Everything after that thought is pure fantasy. Individuals can actually carry on an affair in the mind and emotionally bond to the person of their fantasies.

If we choose plan B, which we will be tempted to, and act upon it for six weeks, we will establish a habit, and the result is a mental stronghold. It is like driving a truck through a pasture for several weeks following the same route. Deep ruts are made when the rain comes. The driver doesn't even need to steer any longer, because the truck will naturally follow those ruts. Any attempt to steer out of them will be met with resistance. Flesh patterns are information pathways in the brain.

Suppose a family has three boys, and the father is a deteriorating alcoholic. Domestic violence plagues the boys, but they all respond differently. The oldest son stands up to his dad, and the middle boy accommodates him. The youngest son runs and hides. Thirty years later, the dad is long gone and the three boys are middle-aged adults. When confronted with a hostile situation, the oldest son will likely stand up and fight, the middle one will accommodate, and the youngest will likely avoid confrontation. That is a stronghold, and there is an infinite number of ways strongholds can be manifested. Tearing down those strongholds and replacing them with truth is a major part of the discipling process.

If we have been trained wrong, can we be retrained? If we programmed our "computer" wrong, can we reprogram it? If we believed a lie, can we renounce that lie and choose to believe the truth? Absolutely, but we have to want to. We are being transformed by the renewing of our minds every time we listen to a good message, read our Bibles, and seek counsel from godly people. But that is not all that is going on. We are not just up against the world and the flesh. We are up against the world, the flesh, and the devil. If we want to mature in Christ, we must reprogram our minds (computers), but we better check for "viruses." Computer viruses are not accidental. They have been maliciously implanted by disgruntled employees and hackers.

Mental strongholds / flesh patterns / defense mechanisms have been developed in our minds, but the verb is present tense in the second half of 2 Corinthians 10:5: "We take captive every thought [*noema*] to make it obedient to Christ." The word *noema* only occurs about six times in Scripture, of which five are in this epistle. It has been translated as "thought," "mind," and "schemes." The way in which the word is used reveals the spiritual battle for our minds. Paul wrote concerning the need to forgive, "I have forgiven in the sight of Christ for your sake, in order that Satan might not outwit us. For we are not unaware of his schemes [*noema*]" (2 Corinthians 2:10–11). We will not be able to set captives free or heal the wounded without helping them forgive others as Christ has forgiven them. Satan will take advantage of our bitterness. We are cautioned not to let a root of bitterness spring up, causing trouble and defiling many (see Hebrews 12:15). Wounds that are not healed are transferred to others.

Concerning salvation, Paul wrote, "[Satan] has blinded the minds [*noema*] of unbelievers, so that they cannot see the light of the gospel that displays the glory of Christ, who is the image of God" (2 Corinthians 4:4; see also 3:14, in which "minds" is also *noema*). We would understand the need for prayer and pray differently if we understood how Satan blinds the minds or thoughts of unbelievers. Evangelism was most effective in the early church when they understood how to free people from demonic influences. Being able to do so became a test of righteousness and orthodoxy (see Luke 9:37–43).

For the fifth usage of *noema* in this epistle, Paul wrote, "I am afraid that just as Eve was deceived by the serpent's cunning, your minds [*noema*] may somehow be led astray from your sincere and pure devotion to Christ" (2 Corinthians 11:3). Satan deceived Eve, and she believed his lies. The tendency is to believe that if we are nice people, such deception can't happen to us, but Eve was *sinless* at the time she was deceived. Good people can be deceived. Please note the spiritual context whenever Paul used the word *noema* in 2 Corinthians.

The final use of the word *noema* is found in Philippians 4:6–7:

> Do not be anxious about anything [i.e., don't be double-minded], but in everything, by prayer and petition, with thanksgiving, present your requests to God. And the peace of God, which transcends all understanding, will guard your hearts and your minds [*noema*] in Christ Jesus.

In order to stand against Satan's mental assaults, we must choose to think on "whatever is true, whatever is noble, whatever is right, whatever is pure, whatever is lovely, whatever is admirable—if anything is excellent or praiseworthy—think about such things" (v. 8). Then we must put our righteous thoughts into practice, "and the God of peace will be with [us]" (v. 9).

In one sense, it doesn't make any difference whether the thoughts are coming from our flesh patterns, from the world, or from the father of lies. We examine every thought, and if it is not true, we don't think it—and we don't believe it. However, it is extremely important that we learn to separate our thoughts from the enemy's thoughts, or we are going to be deceived and defeated. I have discipled hundreds and hundreds of believers who are hearing voices or struggling with condemning and blasphemous thoughts. In almost every case it has proven to be a spiritual battle for their minds. Such people are not going to grow in their faith until that is dealt with through genuine repentance and faith in God, and that includes submitting to God and resisting the devil, in that order (see James 4:7).

I am not the only person seeing this battle for people's minds. All psychiatrists and professional counselors have clients who have these mental struggles. Most would understand such symptoms as the product of a chemical imbalance, but honest questions need to be asked. How can a chemical produce a personality or a thought? How can our neurotransmitters randomly create a thought that we are opposed to thinking? There is no natural explanation. Secularists will likely say that the voices stopped or diminished when the client was given antianxiety medication. That is possible, but so did the whole mental process. All they did was narcotize it. Take away the medication and the thoughts come back. So nothing was cured. It was only covered up. The cause was never determined, and only the symptoms were dealt with. Having no mental peace is a primary reason why people drink or take drugs. You can drown out those thoughts for a short period of time, but reality sets in the next morning.

Can the evil one actually implant a thought in our minds? I wouldn't have had a clue how to answer that question when I was a young pastor, even though I was a graduate from a Bible-believing seminary. Consider the Old Testament passage 1 Chronicles 21:1 (NASB), "Then Satan stood up against Israel and moved David to number Israel." This was no verbal exchange. These were David's thoughts, or at least he thought they were. Satan is not going to try to persuade someone like David, who had a whole heart for God, to sacrifice his babies.

He will try to entice God's people to rely on their resources instead of God's resources—which David did even though the captain of his guard saw it as sin and tried to persuade him otherwise. Thousands died as a result of David's being deceived.

Consider the deception of one of Jesus' own disciples. "And supper being ended, the devil having already put it into the heart of Judas Iscariot, Simon's son, to betray Him . . ." (John 13:2 NKJV). Judas was a thief, and that may be why he was vulnerable, but that flesh pattern does not explain the origin of his plan to betray Jesus. That idea came from Satan. Consider the early church's account of Ananias and Sapphira, who kept for themselves half their profits but wanted the others to think they had given all they had. "Peter said, 'Ananias, why has Satan filled your heart to lie to the Holy Spirit and to keep back some of the price of the land?'" (Acts 5:3 NASB). The word for "filled" in this passage is the same as in Ephesians 5:18, where we are admonished to "be filled with the Spirit." Whatever we yield ourselves to, by that we shall be filled (controlled). If every believer were struck dead for that sin, our churches would be empty. Why the severity of discipline for Ananias and Sapphira? God had to send an early warning to the church, because He knows what the real battle is. If the father of lies can enter your life, marriage, home, or church undetected and persuade you to believe a lie, he could gain some control over your life.

The tendency of the Western church is to dismiss Ananias as an unbeliever, but that is not what the early church believed, nor what present-day scholars believe. F. F. Bruce, a New Testament scholar, wrote that Ananias was a believer.[1] Ernest Haenchen wrote that he was a "Jewish Christian" and commented:

> Satan has filled his heart. Ananias has lied to the Holy Spirit, inasmuch as the Spirit is present in Peter (and in the community). Hence in the last resort it is not simply two men who

confront one another, but in them the Holy Spirit and Satan, whose instruments they are.[2]

The wife of a seminary professor was struggling with pneumonia, and she wasn't responding to treatment. When they removed a liter of fluid from her lungs, they discovered the cancer. She became phobic and asked if I would come to their home to see her. She said, "I'm not sure I'm a Christian." She was a very pious, devoted believer, and I asked why she would even think that way. She said, "I have been struggling with condemning and blasphemous thoughts about God even when I am in church." I asked her, "Did you want to think those thoughts? Did you make a conscious choice to think those thoughts?" She emphatically said no, and I explained, "Then they are not your thoughts." With her maturity it only took a half hour to rid her of those thoughts, and she never questioned her salvation again. She was fearful because she was facing death and questioning her salvation. She wondered, *How can I be a Christian and have those kind of thoughts?* If such thinking came from her core nature, then her salvation would be questionable, but they didn't, and nobody had ever explained that to her. Martin Luther wrote, "The devil throws hideous thoughts into the soul—hatred of God, blasphemy, and despair."[3]

A godly pastor of a four-thousand-member Baptist church had prostate cancer surgery. It was deemed so successful that radiation and chemo weren't considered necessary. He announced that to his congregation, and everyone was thankful. Two months later he was sitting at his desk when the thought came to his mind, *The cancer is back. You're going to die.* He became so fearful that he decided to resign, but before he did he called a pastor friend who advised him to read *Victory Over the Darkness* and *The Bondage Breaker* and meet with an encourager. When the lies were gone, the fear was gone.

How do we make sense of people hearing voices that others don't hear and seeing things that others don't see? In order to physically hear something, there has to be a source for the sound, which produces a compression and rarefaction of air molecules traveling at the speed of sound. Speech cannot be heard in space because sound requires the physical medium of air. The sound hits our eardrums and sends a signal to our brains. In order to physically see something, there has to be a light source reflecting off a material object back to our optic nerve, which sends a signal to our brain. What these people are struggling with cannot be explained in the natural realm: "For our struggle is not against flesh and blood" (Ephesians 6:12 NASB).

On two separate occasions Jesus supernaturally revealed what the Pharisees were doing (see John 7:20–24; John 8:45–59). We know that God is omnipresent and omniscient and knows the thoughts and intentions of our hearts, but the Pharisees didn't know that. For Jesus to have that kind of knowledge, they assumed that He had a demon. Such esoteric knowledge has to have a spiritual origin. In a similar sense, New Agers believe Jesus was the ultimate psychic. Just change the names from demon to spirit guide and medium to psychic, and a gullible public takes the bait.

We have no idea what is going on in the minds of other people, unless they have the courage to reveal it or we have the wisdom to ask the right questions. In our Western culture most are not likely to do so, because they fear being deemed mentally ill and in need of medication, which was the case for the following woman who was on the pastoral staff of a local church:

> I thought my story was unique, but I often wondered if anyone else had the spiritual conflicts I was suffering with. My problem began a couple of years ago. I was experiencing terribly

demonic nightmares and had nights in which I felt the presence of something or someone in my room. One night I woke up feeling like someone was choking me, and I could not speak or say the name of Jesus. I was terrified.

I sought help from church leaders and pastors. They had no idea how to encourage me. Eventually fear turned into panic anxiety disorder, and my thoughts were so loud, destructive, and frightening that I visited my primary care provider. I thought for sure she would understand my belief that this was a spiritual battle. When I expressed the idea that the enemy was attacking me, she responded by diagnosing me with bipolar disorder and told me that I would be on medication for the rest of my life. She also gave me a prescription for antidepressants and antianxiety meds. I was devastated.

I told my husband the diagnosis, and he assured me that it wasn't true. I decided not to take the medication. I just didn't have any peace about it. My pastors prayed over me, but nothing changed. I began Christian counseling, which helped a bit, but it was nowhere near worth the $400 per month that I paid. When I told my Christian counselor about what was happening in my mind, and about my fears, she too said, "I think it is time for medication." It seemed like everyone thought I was crazy. No one believed that my problem was spiritual.

Thankfully, I came across one of your books and read stories of people I could relate to. I knew there was an answer. It was in that book that I first heard of the Steps to Freedom in Christ. Honestly, I was afraid of the Steps at first. I didn't know what to expect, but one of our pastors had recently met Dr. Anderson and was learning how to lead people through the Steps. He offered to help me, and I accepted.

Going through the Steps was one of the most difficult yet incredible things I've ever done. I experienced a lot of interference, such as a headache and confusion, but having the Holy Spirit reveal to me all that I needed to renounce was incredible. When I prayed and asked God to bring to my mind the sins of my ancestors, I was shocked at all that came up. I don't even know my ancestors! I later asked my mother about the things that came to my mind during the session, and she confirmed that my family had been involved in those things. I was amazed by how the Holy Spirit brought out the truth.

After going through the Steps, my mind was completely silent. It was amazing. There were no nagging thoughts. I was totally at peace. I wanted to cry with joy. After that, I wasn't afraid of being alone, and the nightmares were gone. I didn't have to play the radio or television to drown out the terrible thoughts. I could sit in silence and be still.

THREE
Discipleship Counseling

There have been massive cultural changes during my forty years of ministry. The revolution began in the early 1960s. The Vietnam War, free sex, and drugs had a dramatic impact on our culture and the way we did ministry. The family was under siege, and problems arose on a personal level that the church wasn't very well equipped to deal with. In response to the need, Bible colleges and seminaries offered degrees in psychology and marriage and family counseling. There were no seminaries or Christian colleges offering doctoral degrees in psychology in those days, and all the professors had secular degrees. In the following years we experienced a massive growth in such programs, and a corresponding decline in discipleship. It wasn't intentional, but the focus shifted away from repentance and faith in God. It is important to point out that this massive growth in professional counseling is somewhat unique to the United States and Canada, although it is being exported to other countries.

I was speaking to pastors in Palm Springs, California, and Dr. Paul Cedar closed the session by sharing the story of an

African bishop who was visiting the States. In their conversation the bishop asked, "Why do you have so much counseling in your country?" Paul explained that people in our churches have a lot of problems. The bishop said, "Oh, I see. In American you counsel people. In Africa we repent!" An inquirer* told her professional Christian counselor that she was going to visit one of our encouragers to go through a repentance process. The counselor said, "I don't see how repentance can help you." How far have we fallen?

Several years ago Wheaton College conducted a conference on the integration of theology and psychology. Good for them. Half the presenters were theologians and half were psychologists. After the conference, called The Cure of the Soul, the presentations were published in the book *Care for the Soul*. The editors of the book explained the change of title:

> A number of psychologists at the conference expressed discomfort with the grandiosity implied in "The Cure of the Soul." Surely curing the soul is not the job of psychologists. Psychologists treat the soul, easing suffering, helping people in emotional pain to reclaim meaning and purpose and encouraging people to see themselves, others and the world more accurately. In short, psychologists care for the soul. The cure of the soul, most Christian psychologists would suggest, is God's work and is beyond the scope of mainstream psychological interventions."[1]

It is good to recognize our limitations, but if God wants to cure the soul, why are we lowering the bar, especially since God has chosen to work through the church to accomplish that?

Psychology by definition is a study of the soul, and I am certainly not against that. However, I am not in agreement with

* In our ministry we refer to the discipler as an encourager and the one seeking help as an inquirer.

secular psychology in the same way that I am not in agreement with liberal theology. In fact, what is needed is a thoroughly biblical psychology or anthropology, and I know a lot of professional Christian counselors who feel the same way, but where do you go to get it?

A professional counselor attended my class at Talbot School of Theology and said, "I have been counseling people for fifteen years, and I have never seen any evidence of the demonic. However, I have been reading up on the New Age, and I thought I should be prepared in case I happen to come across it in my office." A month later he wrote me a letter and stated that all his clients were being deceived, and so was he. Why didn't he see it before? Most professional counselors are trained to analyze, understand, explain, and help people cope with their problems. The devil couldn't care less and will continue his covert activities. The first objective of Satan is to remain hidden. The true nature of the conflict becomes apparent when lies are exposed and when inquirers are working toward resolution.

The same is true for pastors. If all we are doing is preaching and teaching, it is unlikely that we will see any demonic manifestations or be aware of any spiritual opposition. Meanwhile, the client and the people in the pews are struggling mightily with their thoughts. I asked a pastor who oversaw this ministry in a large church that has led thousands through the Steps to Freedom, "Knowing what you know now, and what you knew ten years ago, what is your take on the average church in America?" He said, "Pastors don't have a clue what is going on in the minds of their people."

I certainly didn't realize the battle for people's minds when I was a pastor. After a morning service a middle-aged man privately said to me, "Pastor, I have this voice in my head." I had no idea what that was, and even if I did, I wouldn't have known what to do about it. So I helplessly watched his marriage and family fall apart and leave the church. My first attempt to disciple a man in his twenties ended in frustration. I only learned two years later that his mind was consumed with lust.

After attending a Discipleship Counseling conference, a young man said he had just enrolled in a secular five-year doctor of psychology program and asked me if I thought that was advisable. I said, "I am not going to suggest how God is leading you, but I wouldn't spend $200,000 and five years of my life learning how to help people live independently of God and see that their needs are met without Christ." He said, "I never thought about it that way." Isn't that what they are doing? Secular psychology makes sense if you are only dealing with natural people who are living in a natural world excluded from the reality of the spiritual world, which of course is impossible.

Including God

What sets Christian ministry apart from secular counseling and mentoring is a Christian worldview and the inclusion of God in the process. Since God is omnipresent, we have to understand what our role relationship is with God. I believe that in God's wisdom there is a precise line between God's sovereignty and human responsibility. The line will be a little blurred for us, and the Calvinist and the Armenian will adjust the line to the left or to the right. Both theological perspectives, however, acknowledge that Scripture teaches God's sovereignty and human responsibility. On the left side of the line is what God, and only God, can do. We can be creative, but we can't speak and bring something into existence out of nothing. We can't even save ourselves. God created the universe, and He accomplishes His purposes by working through His created order. The providence of God refers to His direction and care over all creation. God "upholds all things by the word of His power" (Hebrews 1:3).

He is the ultimate reality, and if He disappeared so would all creation. We fulfill our purpose when we live in harmony with Him. We do that by knowing Him and His ways and living accordingly by faith.

God's Sovereignty | Human Responsibility

Everything on the right side of the line depicts human responsibility. I do not believe that we can pray and ask God to do for us what He told us to do. If you have an important exam tomorrow, you can't ask God to study for you. He told you to study in order to present yourself approved to God as a workman who does not need to be ashamed (see 2 Timothy 2:15). You can't ask God to think for you, because He told us "to think so as to have sound judgment" (Romans 12:3). We have to assume our responsibility for our own attitudes and actions. Suppose there is a problem person in your church, and some well-meaning Christians ask God to remove him from your fellowship, but nothing happens. *Why not, God? Don't you love your church?* The church is His body, which Jesus paid the ultimate price for, but God told us to go to such a person in private for the purpose of restoration; if the person doesn't repent, then bring two more witnesses to confront him. The person should be removed from fellowship if there is no repentance. Will God bail us out if we don't do that? I have not seen it.

Suppose a person is frightened by some spiritual manifestation in her room and cries out, "God, do something," and nothing happens. So the person hides under the covers and wonders, *Why not, God? You are all powerful. Why won't you help me? Don't you love me? Maybe I'm not a Christian, and that is why God doesn't answer.* That is the mental and emotional state of most people I have worked with. They are questioning God's presence, questioning His love for them, and questioning their salvation. But why didn't God do something? He did. He disarmed the devil, forgave our sins, made us new creations in Christ, and positioned us with Christ in the heavenlies at the Father's right hand. Whose responsibility is it to submit to God and resist the devil? Who's responsibility is it to put on the armor of God, take every thought captive to the obedience of Christ, stand firm in our faith, and make no provision for the flesh in regard to its lusts? Can we assume that there will be no negative consequences if we don't assume our responsibility? Will God bail us out if we don't? I have not seen it!

Who Is Responsible for What?

When I am asked to help another individual, I do so with the awareness that God is always present and that there is a role that God, and only God, can play in the other person's life. On the right side of the line in the above diagram, there is another role relationship that exists, and that is between the encourager and the inquirer, the discipler and the disciple. Think of it as a triangle with God at the top:

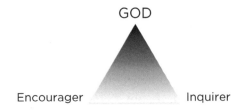

GOD

Encourager   Inquirer

Each side of the triangle represents a relationship. The most important one is my own relationship with God. I need to make sure that the barriers to an intimate relationship with God have been removed through my own repentance. It is also very important how I relate to the inquirer. Secular counselors focus all their attention on that relationship, because their relationship with God and that of their client's relationship with God is never even considered. Most have learned how not to be a rescuer, an enabler, or a codependent. They have also developed skills like accurate empathy, congruence, genuineness, and concreteness. Those are good pastoral skills that we can learn from, but they have left out God.

With the triangle in mind, consider who is responsible for what. A lot of problems in our homes, marriages, and ministries would disappear if we had a balanced answer to that question. Have you ever tried to play the role of the Holy Spirit in the life of your spouse? Your staff? An inquirer? How did that work for you? There is a role that God, and only God, can play in the life of another, and we will foul up the process if we usurp His role. Have you ever tried to assume another person's responsibility? They won't think or make a decision, so you do their thinking and deciding for them. Now they are dependent upon you instead of God.

What are we actually trying to accomplish? What is the primary ministry of the church? I believe Paul answers the question in 2 Corinthians 5:17–18: "Therefore if anyone is in Christ, he is a new creature; the old things passed away; behold, new things have come. Now all these things are from God, who reconciled us to Himself through Christ and gave us the ministry of reconciliation." In other words, the ministry of those who are reconciled to God is to help others to be reconciled to God—i.e., to have an intimate relationship with their heavenly Father through genuine repentance and faith in God. Discipleship is a ministry of reconciliation. The whole world is in a mess because of the fall, and God has only one plan A, and that is to reestablish fallen humanity and present them complete in Christ (see Colossians 1:28). Jesus said, "The time is fulfilled, and the kingdom of God is at hand; repent and believe the gospel" (Mark 1:15). The big question is this: Do we really believe that repentance and faith in God are the means by which we resolve personal and spiritual conflicts? The answer is *no* if we usurp each other's roles and fail to include God in the process. The answer is *yes* if we acknowledge God's role and assume responsibility for ours.

Inquirer's Responsibility

We can't do anything about the sovereignty of God other than to teach it and rest in the finished work of Christ. Rest assured that God will always do His part, so the remaining question is the role responsibilities of the inquirer (disciple) and the encourager (discipler). To separate the two roles, consider the passage in James 5:13–16. The tendency for people in ministry is to see this passage from their perspective and see only the role of the righteous man. What gets overlooked is the responsibility of the one seeking help, and if not assumed, the prayers of righteous people will not accomplish much (see v. 16).

The passage begins with "Is anyone among you suffering? Then he must pray." Initially, the one who should be praying is the inquirer. Why? Because nobody else can do their praying for them. Please don't misunderstand me. I believe in intercessory prayer, but that was never meant to replace an individual's responsibility to pray. Christians are children of God, and they all have the same access to their heavenly Father. To illustrate, suppose a father has two sons, and the younger brother is always asking his older brother to go to their father on his behalf and ask for money or whatever. No good father would accept a secondhand relationship with his children. Surely he would say, "Go tell your brother to come see me himself."

God was sending all kinds of hurting people to me when I taught at Talbot School of Theology. Inevitably I would get stuck while trying to help them, so I would tell inquirers, "I don't know how to help you, but I know God does. So I am going to pray and ask God for wisdom, which we are told to do in James 1:5." Many times I would sit in silence and wait for the Lord to enlighten me. Then one day I realized I was asking God to tell me so that I could tell the inquirer. That would make me a medium, and there is only "one mediator also between God and men, the man Christ Jesus" (1 Timothy 2:5). So rather than my trying to do their praying for them, I had them pray, and my effectiveness in ministry changed forever.

One afternoon I wrote out seven simple petitions that inquirers could pray, and I tried it out with several people. Frankly, I was astonished to learn how effective that was. When they asked God to reveal to their minds whom they needed to forgive, names of people surfaced who hadn't been a part of our conversation until then. Eventually those prayers became the Steps to Freedom in Christ. The repentance was genuine and the results lasted, because God was leading the process and the inquirers were doing the repenting. I was just facilitating a ministry of reconciliation.

Suppose you are attempting to disciple a male college student. On your first meeting he shares about the dysfunctional home he was raised in, which was headed by his abusive father. He is depressed and lethargic about school. Undoubtedly he has a poor self-image, but that is a symptom and not the cause. Most presenting problems are symptomatic, which professional counselors are fully aware of. A major goal of psychotherapy is to identify root causes. A good pastor should know that forgiving his father is an essential step for the student in setting himself free from his past and moving forward. Suppose you helped him do that. You have done a good work, and you would likely see a positive change in his countenance, but have you done enough? If he prayed and asked God to reveal to his mind whom he needed to forgive, he will likely mention his father first, but chances are another twenty or more names will come to his mind. What if he forgives his father, but not the other twenty? What are the chances that he has been sexually active? That he has been rebellious? Used drugs? Will he become a fruitful disciple if those issues aren't dealt with?

These are God's children we are working with, and God knows everything about them. God will convict them of sin, so we don't have to do that. I don't point out sin in other people, because I have found it to be counterproductive. It misdirects their battles with God onto me. When conviction comes from God, the power to change comes with it. When they pray and ask God to reveal to their minds how they have been misguided, deceived, rebellious, prideful, etc., it is amazing what surfaces. We commonly hear inquirers say, "I have never shared this with anyone ever before." Such revelations have very little to do with our unique abilities. They have petitioned God, and He is surfacing all the issues that need to be resolved.

I have asked leaders all over the world three questions. First, "How many of you would be willing to share all the dirt in your lives just for the purpose of sharing it?" Nobody raises their hand, except for an occasional exhibitionist. Second, "How many would be willing to share all the dirt in your lives for the purpose of gaining some understanding as to why you are all screwed up?" A few will raise their hands, but even then somewhat reluctantly. That is as far as secular counseling can take anyone. The goal is to develop trusting relationships and draw as much information as possible out of their clients and explain why they are feeling and acting the way they are. They can't go any further than that without the gospel. Without the gospel we are just products of our past, and we would need to learn how to live with that reality.

Third, "How many of you would be willing to share all the dirt in your lives in order to resolve it?" Everyone's hand goes up. We are not just products of our past. We are new creations in Christ. I can't fix your past, and God doesn't either. He sets you free from it. God is bringing to mind all the issues that are keeping you from having an intimate relationship with your heavenly Father. Resolution is taking place the moment they begin the repentance process.

James continues, "Is anyone among you sick? Then he must call for the elders of the church" (5:14). God puts the responsibility on the one seeking help to take the initiative. We will never see wholeness, health, and freedom in our churches unless we help people realize that gaining such is their responsibility. We can't be healthy for other people. We can't repent or believe for them, but godly elders can help them and be equipped to offer them that opportunity.

James adds another qualifier, "Therefore, confess your sins to one another, and pray for one another so that you may be healed. The effective prayer of a righteous man can accomplish much" (v. 16). The prayer of a righteous person doesn't accomplish much until the person being prayed for is right with God. Suppose a person in your church calls the elders for prayer, and the elders take that responsibility very seriously. They agree to fast for a day before they anoint the person with oil and fervently pray for a healing. Later they discover that the person is in bondage to bitterness and has many other unresolved spiritual issues. Should we expect God to answer those prayers? I don't think so. If we really cared for such people, we would help them resolve those conflicts first. Then watch how effective our prayers become.

A desperate woman asked for some of my time, which I gave her. She said she had deep spiritual conflicts. After sharing her story she said, "God promised prosperity and good health in 3 John 2. Why isn't that happening?" I said, "You should finish the verse—'just as your soul prospers.' You shared with me that you have had two abortions and years of drug abuse. How do you think your soul is doing?" I have also seen a similar faulty perspective derived from Psalm 37:4: "Delight yourself in the Lord; and He will give you the desires of your heart." Can't you just hear someone say, "Claim that promise, folks. God is going to give you the desires of your heart if you will only believe. So name it and claim it, but you won't get what you want if you don't believe hard enough." If you delight yourselves in the Lord, your desires will change. If you don't first delight yourselves in the Lord, your desires will be of the flesh, and they cannot be satisfied.

Encourager's Responsibility

One of the best passages describing the role of the encourager is 2 Timothy 2:24–26:

> The Lord's bond-servant must not be quarrelsome, but be kind to all, able to teach, patient when wronged, with gentleness correcting those who are in opposition, if perhaps God may grant them repentance leading to the knowledge of the truth, and they may come to their senses and escape from the snare of the devil, having been held captive by him to do his will.

People's lives are like a house where the garbage hasn't been taken out in months. That is going to attract a lot of flies. It is understandable why the natural response is to get rid of the flies, but what we really should get rid of is the garbage. I am well aware that some ministries study the flight patterns of the flies, try to get their names and rank, and attempt to cast them out. There may be some value in doing that, which I am not aware of, but I believe that repentance and faith in God has been and will continue to be the answer throughout the church age.

One can chase off the flies, but they will likely tell seven others where the garbage is.

The encourager only has to work with the inquirer, and can do so without any demons manifesting themselves. Our goal is for God to manifest himself, and then He is glorified. To accomplish this we must be the Lord's bond-servant; i.e., we must be totally dependent upon God. Discipleship counseling is an encounter with God. He is the one who grants repentance, and God is the only One who can set captives free and heal the wounds of the brokenhearted. We have to avoid being quarrelsome, and be kind, patient, and gentle. We also have to know the truth, because truth sets us free.

I have often been asked how we can know whether a problem is spiritual or psychological. The question implies a false dichotomy. It is never either/or. It is always both/and. Our soul is always part of the equation, and God is always present. There is no time and place where it is safe to take off the armor of God. Our only sanctuary is our position in Christ, not some physical location. There is always the possibility of being tempted, accused, and deceived. We have a whole God who takes into account all reality all the time. Believing that will keep us from polarizing into psychotherapeutic ministries that ignore the reality of the spiritual world or some kind of deliverance-only ministry. The devil isn't the issue. The real issue is our relationship with God.

If you are unfamiliar with this perspective, you have to be wondering if this approach really works. There have been several exploratory studies that have shown promising results regarding the effectiveness of the Steps to Freedom in Christ. In 1996, Christian therapist Judith King did three pilot studies with participants who attended a Living Free in Christ conference[†]

† The Living Free in Christ conference is now available as curriculum: *Freedom in Christ Small-Group Bible Study Leader's Guide* contains all the messages written out, which the leaders can teach themselves; *Freedom in Christ Small-Group Bible*

and were led through the Steps to Freedom in Christ during the conference. In each case, participants completed a questionnaire before working through the Steps. Three months afterward, the participants filled out the same questionnaire again. The questionnaires assessed for levels of depression, anxiety, inner conflict, tormenting thoughts, and addictive behaviors.[2]

The following table illustrates the percentage of improvement for each category:

	Pilot Study 1	Pilot Study 2	Pilot Study 3
Depression	64%	47%	52%
Anxiety	58%	44%	47%
Inner Conflict	63%	51%	48%
Tormenting Thoughts	82%	58%	57%
Addictive Behavior	52%	43%	39%

Most people attending a Living Free in Christ conference can work through the repentance process on their own using the Steps to Freedom in Christ. In our experience, about 15 percent can't, because of difficulties they have experienced. A personal session with a trained encourager was offered to them.

At two conferences, people who had sessions with trained encouragers were given a pre-test before a Step session and a post-test three months later. All the encouragers were well-trained laypeople. There was not one professional pastor or counselor involved in the research. The participants showed the following improvements in seven key categories:[3]

Study Student's Guide is for each participant and includes the Steps to Freedom in Christ; and *Freedom in Christ Small-Group Bible Study DVD* features my teaching of the twelve messages, for leaders who prefer the course to be taught that way (all from Bethany House Publishers, 2008).

	Conference 1	Conference 2
Depression	44%	52%
Anxiety	45%	44%
Fear	48%	49%
Anger	36%	55%
Tormenting Thoughts	51%	27%
Negative Habits	48%	43%
Sense of Self-Worth	52%	40%

I was asked to teach a doctor of ministry class at Regent University. The one-week intensive was also attended by masters of divinity and doctor of psychology students, swelling the number to over forty. Dr. Fernando Garzon, a professor of psychology at Regent University at the time, asked if I would be willing to let the students take a pre-test and post-test, using clinical scales that measured levels of anxiety and depression. I did so with the understanding that such students don't represent the general population, since they were all committed Christians working on post-graduate degrees. They took the tests Monday morning and were taught the core message of Freedom in Christ Ministries. They were led through the Steps to Freedom in Christ and took the same tests again at the end of the class. Their post-assignment was to read *Walking in Freedom*, which is a twenty-one-day devotional that we recommend inquirers read after a freedom appointment. Then they were administered the same tests for a third time, three weeks after the class.

Every scale was statistically significant, and the results lasted. Dr. Garzon wrote an article sharing the results and submitted it to the *Journal of Psychology and Theology*.[4] They ran the article and asked Dr. Garzon, "How does Dr. Anderson explain such results? What is he doing beyond cognitive behavioral therapy?" It is a fair question. I taught the truth to the best of my ability, and the truth set them free. End of story, or was it? Dr. Garzon, who presently teaches at Liberty University, called me and asked how I would answer that question. I told him that three issues come to mind.

First, even if cognitive behavior therapy is conducted by committed Christians using the truth of God's Word as their base, it will not be lastingly effective without the presence of Christ. Applying the words of Christ without the life of Christ is not just an issue for Christian counselors; it is a problem that plagues the church. Dead orthodoxy is dead. Nothing grows without life. Our ministry is to connect people to God, not just provide information about Him.

> For the word of God is living and active and sharper than any two-edged sword, and piercing as far as the division of soul and spirit, of both joints and marrow, and able to judge the thoughts and intentions of the heart. And there is no creature hidden from His sight, but all things are open and laid bare to the eyes of Him with whom we have to do.
>
> Hebrews 4:12–13

Which "word" are they talking about? The notes in my *Ryrie Study Bible* say, "*The Word of God.* Here meaning His inspired Word, the Scriptures."[5] The following are the notes in *The Orthodox Study Bible*: "The phrase *His sight* (v. 13) tells us this reference is not to the written word, Holy Scripture, but to the Word of God Himself, our Lord Jesus Christ (see John 1:1–18). Nothing is able to escape the discernment of Christ, the Word of God."[6] In this case the Orthodox are right. The previous context in Hebrews presented Jesus as greater than Moses and the angels. I always have my Bible with me, and divine revelation is the basis for all that I believe, but what makes our ministry effective is the presence of God. Words in my Bible don't judge the thoughts and intentions of the heart. God does.

Jesus is the Truth and the Word, and when we use God's Word as an intellectual pursuit of knowledge, it is no longer living. Christianity is not an intellectual pursuit. It is a personal relationship with God. We must keep in mind that "knowledge makes arrogant, but love edifies" (1 Corinthians 8:1). When we make knowledge an end in itself, we undermine the purpose for which it was intended. "The goal of our instruction is love from a pure heart and a good conscience and a sincere faith" (1 Timothy 1:5). One can know theology and be arrogant, but we can't know God and be arrogant. "All Scripture is inspired by God and profitable for teaching, for reproof, for correction, for training in righteousness" (2 Timothy 3:16). Too often we have used it for teaching and training in competence. There will be no righteousness without reproof and correction, and that happens when it is God who is granting repentance. God told Moses, "My presence shall go with you, and I will give you rest" (Exodus 33:14). The Great Commission to make disciples comes with the assurance that "I am with you always, even to the end of the age" (Matthew 28:20). We make every effort to practice the presence of God when we disciple others.

Second, cognitive behavioral therapy that does not take into account the reality of the spiritual world will again fall far short of its potential. We can't usurp the role of the Holy Spirit, who will convict us of sin and lead us into all truth. Nor should we overlook the possibility that an individual could be paying attention to a deceiving spirit (see 1 Timothy 4:1).

Third, I am not the Wonderful Counselor. God is. I didn't change their lives. God did. I was just an instrument in His hands trying my best to reconcile children of God with their heavenly Father.

FOUR
A Strategy for Making Reproducible Disciples

Throughout the 1990s I asked pastors how many people in their churches know who they are in Christ, know what it means to be a child of God, have a devotional and prayer life, and are bearing fruit. I never had one pastor guesstimate more than 15 percent. Since the beginning of the third millennium most have said 5 percent. It is not for lack of resources, because there is an abundance of books, videos, and curriculum, and most of it is available on a smartphone. Paul comments on such carnality in 1 Corinthians 3:1–3 (emphasis added):

> And I, brethren, could not speak to you as to spiritual men, but as to men of flesh, as to *infants in Christ*. I gave you milk to drink, not solid food; for you were *not able to receive it*. Indeed, even now you are not yet able, for you are still fleshly. For since there is jealously and strife among you, are you not fleshly, and are you not walking like mere men?

We will continue to have "infants in Christ," sitting in our churches "not able to receive" good messages unless there is some way to resolve such conflicts; hence the need for genuine repentance.

I have seen inquirers in my office who are unable to receive what I'm sharing. One said to me later, "I saw your lips move, but I didn't hear a word you were saying." I sent a man a set of CDs to listen to as he drove four hours to meet with me. He handed me the CDs saying they were all blank. I led him through the Steps to Freedom in Christ, and he listened to the same set all the way home. Have you ever read a chapter in your Bible and asked yourself, "What did I just read?" Then you read the same chapter again and the same thing happened again? Did that ever happen when you read the sports page or gossip column in your daily paper? Messages given on Sunday mornings are going right over the heads of many attendees. Many have told me that they stopped reading their Bibles because all they saw was condemnation. In *The Steps to Freedom in Christ* book I include a "Statements of Truth" section, which is just a collection of Scripture verses. Many will read it but make no connection to the truth it conveys. Some have said, "I'm just reading words." When they have finished the Steps, I will have them return to that page and read it again. This time they connect, and usually a big smile appears on their faces. Now they can read their Bibles with comprehension. I have asked many, "Now, when you read your Bible, what do you see?" Almost all will say, "I'm in Christ! Why couldn't I see that before?" Before repentance there was no growth, but now they devour their Bibles and their spiritual growth accelerates.

Paul and John present three levels of growth from different perspectives. John wrote,

I am writing to you, little children, because your sins have been forgiven you for His name's sake. I am writing to you, fathers, because you know Him who has been from the beginning. I am writing to you, young men, because you have overcome the evil one. I have written to you, children, because you know the

Father. I have written to you, fathers, because you know Him who has been from the beginning. I have written to you, young men, because you are strong, and the word of God abides in you, and you have overcome the evil one.

1 John 2:12–14

Little children have an elementary knowledge of who their Father is, and they have overcome the penalty of sin. Fathers have a much deeper experiential and reverential relationship with their heavenly Father, whom they have known from the beginning. Young men in the faith have "overcome the evil one," which John repeats twice. They have overcome the power of sin. They no longer have any uncontrollable appetites or addictive behaviors, and have overcome the barriers preventing them from having an intimate relationship with their heavenly Father. How are we going to help our people reach the stature of "young men" if they don't know how to overcome the evil one?

Paul outlines the maturation process in Colossians 2:6–7:

Therefore as you have received Christ Jesus the Lord, so walk in Him, having been firmly rooted and now being built up in Him and established in your faith, just as you were instructed, and overflowing with gratitude.

New believers must first become firmly rooted in Christ in order for them to grow in Christ, and live freely in Christ. The next verse is a parenthetical insertion describing how not to make fruitful disciples:

See to it that no one takes you captive through philosophy and empty deception, according to the tradition of men, according to the elementary principles of the world, rather than according to Christ.

v. 8

Then Paul comes back to the core issue of Christianity:

> For in Him all the fullness of Deity dwells in bodily form, and in Him you have been made complete, and He is the head over all rule and authority.
>
> vv. 9–10

Every aspect of our growth in Christ is dependent upon our union with God. The following chart illustrates what obstacles need to be overcome and what lessons need to be learned at various stages of growth—spiritually, rationally, emotionally, volitionally, and relationally.

LEVELS OF CONFLICT

	Level One *Rooted in Christ*	Level Two *Built up in Christ*	Level Three *Living in Christ*
Spiritual	Lack of salvation or assurance • Ephesians 2:1–3	Living according to the flesh • Galatians 5:19–21	Insensitive to the Spirit's leading • Hebrews 5:11–14
Rational	Pride and ignorance • 1 Corinthians 8:1	Wrong belief or philosophy • Colossians 2:8	Lack of knowledge • Hosea 4:6
Emotional	Fearful, guilty, and shameful • Matthew 10:26–33 • Romans 3:23	Angry, anxious, and depressed • Ephesians 4:31 • 1 Peter 5:7 • 2 Corinthians 4:1–18	Discouraged and sorrowful • Galatians 6:9
Volitional	Rebellious • 1 Timothy 1:9	Lack of self-control • 1 Corinthians 3:1–3	Undisciplined • 2 Thessalonians 3:7, 11
Relational	Rejected and unloved • 1 Peter 2:4	Bitter and unforgiving • Colossians 3:13	Selfish • 1 Corinthians 10:24 • Philippians 2:1–5

New believers can sit under the teaching of the best Bible teachers and make no progress at all if they don't have a clue who they are in Christ and struggle with pride, guilt, shame, fear, rebellion, bitterness, and interpersonal conflicts. The purpose of discipleship counseling is to resolve the personal and spiritual conflicts that are keeping them from being firmly rooted in Christ. Once they are resolved, the growth process is uninhibited. Leading someone through the Steps to Freedom in Christ is not an end; it is a beginning of the growth process. The following chart illustrates the growth and functional capability at each level of maturity:

LEVELS OF GROWTH

	Level One *Rooted in Christ*	Level Two *Built up in Christ*	Level Three *Living in Christ*
Spiritual	Child of God • Romans 8:16	Lives according to the Spirit • Galatians 5:22–23	Led by the Spirit • Romans 8:14
Rational	Knows the truth • John 8:32	Correctly uses the Bible • 2 Timothy 2:15	Adequate and equipped • 2 Timothy 3:16–17
Emotional	Free • Galatians 5:1	Joyful, peaceful, and patient • Galatians 5:22	Contented • Philippians 4:11
Volitional	Submissive • Romans 13:1–5	Self-controlled • Galatians 5:23	Disciplined • 1 Timothy 4:7–8
Relational	Accepted and forgiven • Romans 5:8; 15:7	Forgiving • Ephesians 4:32	Loving and unselfish • Philippians 2:1–5

When applied to believers, salvation is presented in past, present, and future tenses in the Bible. We have been saved (see Ephesians 2:5, 8; 2 Timothy 1:8–9), we are presently being saved (1 Corinthians 1:18; 2 Corinthians 2:15), and someday we shall be fully saved (Romans 5:9–10; 13:11). For believers, our salvation experience is not yet fully complete, and it won't be until we physically die, receive a resurrected body, and reside fully in the presence of God. God does, however, desire for us to presently have the assurance of salvation (see 1 John 5:13). There is a "coming wrath" (see 1 Thessalonians 1:10) of God, but we have the assurance that when that wrath comes, we will be saved from it, having believed: "You were sealed *in Him* with the Holy Spirit of promise, who is given as a pledge of our inheritance, with a view to the redemption of God's own possession, to the praise of His glory" (Ephesians 1:13–14).

I heard a man boast that he was saved, sealed, and sanctified, implying that there was nothing more he needed to do. For him salvation and sanctification were both complete. He is not alone in that assessment. Many believers think they have been saved fully in the past, and that is all that has to happen. Such erroneous thinking doesn't provide very much motivation to press on in the pursuit of God, as the apostle Paul exhorted us to do in Philippians 3:13–14:

> Brethren, I do not regard myself as having laid hold of it yet; but one thing I do: forgetting what lies behind and reaching forward to what lies ahead, I press on toward the goal for the prize of the upward call of God in Christ Jesus.

If you have been born again, you are indeed in the kingdom of God, but you will likely be stagnant in your growth if you fail to "work out your salvation with fear and trembling" (Philippians 2:12). Notice that you don't work for your salvation, which is a free gift of God appropriated by faith. We all need to work out in our experience what God has worked in us. Beyond our initial salvation experience, God's will for our lives is our sanctification (see 1 Thessalonians 4:3), which also occurs in Scripture in past, present, and future tenses when applied to believers. In other words believers have been sanctified (see 1 Corinthians 1:2; 6:11), they are being sanctified (2 Corinthians 7:1; 1 Thessalonians 4:3), and someday they will be fully sanctified (1 Thessalonians 3:12–13; 5:23–24). The sanctifying process begins at our new birth and ends in glorification. The author of Hebrews wrote, "Make every effort to live in peace with all men and to be holy; without holiness no one will see the Lord" (Hebrews 12:14 NIV1984).

Past-tense sanctification is referred to by theologians as positional sanctification, and present tense sanctification is referred to as progressive sanctification. Holiness churches tend to focus on positional sanctification, and many of them see sanctification as a done deal, which can lead to serious errors. One man boasted that he hadn't sinned in twenty years. I asked him if his wife would agree with that assessment. The apostle John wrote, "If we say that we have no sin, we are deceiving ourselves and the truth is not in us" (1 John 1:8).

Reformed theology tends to focus on progressive sanctification, which makes sanctification synonymous with growth or maturity. Positional sanctification is often dismissed by some as just positional truth, as though it is practically irrelevant. Consequently, many are trying to become someone they already are. Positional sanctification is the basis for progressive sanctification. Christians are not trying to become children of God; they are children of God who are in the process of becoming like Christ. Positional sanctification (who we already are in Christ) is the basis for progressive sanctification (becoming like Christ).

Entrance Into the Church

Entrance into the early church began with a repentance process followed by baptism. They would literally face the west and renounce Satan and all his works and all his ways. Then they would face the east and make their profession of faith in Christ. Catholic and Orthodox churches still follow that procedure, but it has been considerably minimalized. There are some older protestant liturgical churches that still follow that practice as well. The purpose was to publicly say in essence, "I used to believe a certain way and live accordingly, but now I renounce those beliefs and that way of life. I now choose to trust God, believe His Word, and live accordingly." If their faith was sincere and their repentance genuine, there would be an observable change in their lives and how they lived.

Entrance into most evangelical churches begins with a salvation experience that would appear more like addition than transformation, which is what salvation really is. They just received Christ and added Him onto their lives. Without repentance, they still believe what they have always believed, but now they also believe something new as well. We can't believe the truth and a lie at the same time and expect to grow. If I choose to believe the truth, then there should be a corresponding choice to no longer believe the lies. "You cannot drink the cup of the Lord and the cup of demons; you cannot partake of the table of the Lord and the table of demons" (1 Corinthians 10:21). All children of God are positionally alive and free in Christ, but how many are living that way? If they want to experience that freedom and grow in the grace and knowledge of the Lord Jesus Christ, they need to repent.

Where Do We Start?

Very little training is required for mature and biblically literate pastors to lead an inquirer through the Steps to Freedom in Christ. It is actually a self-guided tour that people can process on their own. I have received emails and letters from people all over the world who have processed the Steps on their own. Dr. Wayne Grudem is the most read systematic theologian in the world today, and in my estimation a very godly man. In the foreword for my book *Liberating Prayer*, which includes the Steps, Dr. Grudem wrote:

> After living more than 50 years as a Christian, and after teaching more than 25 years as a professor of Bible and theology, I took about two hours to work carefully through Neil's seven "Steps to Freedom in Christ" and apply each step to my own life, reading each suggested prayer aloud. God used that process to bring to mind a number of thoughts and attitudes that He wanted to correct, and then to impart to me a wonderfully refreshing sense of freedom, peace, joy, and fellowship with Himself.[1]

In most cases we just show up, and God sets them free. However, there are difficult cases that require some training. The purpose of Freedom in Christ Ministries is to equip the church worldwide, enabling them to establish their people, marriages, and ministries alive and free in Christ through genuine repentance and faith in God. We are not a counseling ministry, and we will not do your discipling for you, but we will help you equip godly people in your church who can help others. We have offices and representatives around the world who will offer that kind of training for a select few in your church. Our office in the United States has an online university that people in your church can enroll in, and be a part of our Community Freedom Ministry (see www.ficm.org). There are hundreds of such associates in the United States and Canada. We require three of my books to be read: *Victory Over the Darkness*, *The Bondage Breaker*, and *Discipleship Counseling*. Having trained encouragers in a church takes a huge load off the pastor.

For the congregation we offer *Freedom in Christ Small-Group Bible Study*, a basic discipleship course and curriculum that explains creation, the fall, worldview, how to live by faith, mental strongholds, the battle for our minds, emotions, forgiveness, and relational perspectives.* There is also a British edition taught by Steve Goss, our international director. This course has been translated into many languages (see www.ficminter national.org). Youth for Christ has partnered with our ministry to produce *Freedom in Christ for Young People*, curriculum for both junior high and high school students.

The best possible scenario is to plant a church and offer the class for all new members. Imagine a church where everyone knows who they are in Christ and has resolved all known personal and spiritual conflicts. However, it is never too late to offer the class in Sunday school, fellowship groups, and home Bible studies. But it can't be a onetime offering, because every church has a constant turnover of people. The class should be continually offered for new members and converts.

Overcoming Flesh Patterns

The purpose of the Freedom in Christ course is to establish participants alive and free in Christ by submitting to God and resisting the devil (see James 4:7). Rich Miller, president of Freedom in Christ Ministries—USA, and I have written the twenty-one-day devotional *Walking in Freedom*. Each day has truth about God, truth about who we are in Christ, and truth about freedom. Every third day, readers are encouraged to go through one of the seven Steps to reinforce what they have previously done. Once the barriers are removed between them and God, the life of Christ will empower them to grow and bear fruit. With a quiet and clear mind they are able to be transformed by the renewing of their minds. Some, however, will have major flesh patterns that need

*For a full description of the curriculum, see footnote in chapter 3 (page 67) and the Books and Resources section in the back of this book.

to be crucified (see Galatians 5:24). Chief among them are anger, sexual strongholds, chemical addiction, depression, and anxiety disorders, as well as the need to set marriages and ministries free through corporate repentance. The rest of this book includes chapters covering each of those issues. Ideally, a church could offer a support group for such personal needs, but if that is not available, I have written a book for each of those issues that can be kept in the church library or made available for loan or purchase.

Finally, I have written THE VICTORY SERIES, a comprehensive discipleship course to be used after the basic discipleship course. It follows the flow of being rooted in Christ, growing in Christ, living in Christ, and overcoming in Christ. The series includes the following eight books, with each session having five lessons (240 total) that conclude with study questions and a quote from one of the early church fathers:

Study 1 *God's Story for You: Discover the Person*
        God Created You to Be

Session One: The Story of Creation
Session Two: The Story of the Fall
Session Three: The Story of Salvation
Session Four: The Story of God's Sanctification
Session Five: The Story of God's Transforming Power
Session Six: The Story of God

Study 2 *Your New Identity: A Transforming Union With God*

Session One: A New Life "in Christ"
Session Two: A New Understanding of God's Character
Session Three: A New Understanding of God's Nature
Session Four: A New Relationship With God
Session Five: A New Humanity
Session Six: A New Beginning

Study 3   *Your Foundation in Christ: Live by the Power of the Spirit*
Session One: Liberating Truth
Session Two: The Nature of Faith
Session Three: Living Boldly
Session Four: Godly Relationships
Session Five: Freedom of Forgiveness
Session Six: Living by the Spirit

Study 4   *Renewing Your Mind: Become More Like Christ*
Session One: Being Transformed
Session Two: Living Under Grace
Session Three: Overcoming Anger
Session Four: Overcoming Anxiety
Session Five: Overcoming Depression
Session Six: Overcoming Losses

Study 5   *Growing in Christ: Deepen Your Relationship With Jesus*
Session One: Spiritual Discernment
Session Two: Spiritual Gifts
Session Three: Growing Through Committed Relationships
Session Four: Overcoming Sexual Bondage
Session Five: Overcoming Chemical Addiction
Session Six: Suffering for Righteousness' Sake

Study 6   *Your Life in Christ: Walk in Freedom by Faith*
Session One: God's Will
Session Two: Faith Appraisal (Part 1)
Session Three: Faith Appraisal (Part 2)

Session Four: Spiritual Leadership
Session Five: Discipleship Counseling
Session Six: The Kingdom of God

Study 7   *Your Authority in Christ: Overcoming Strongholds in Your Life*
Session One: The Origin of Evil
Session Two: Good and Evil Spirits
Session Three: Overcoming the Opposition
Session Four: Kingdom Sovereignty
Session Five: The Armor of God (Part 1)
Session Six: The Armor of God (Part 2)

Study 8   *Your Ultimate Victory: Standing Strong in the Faith*
Session One: The Battle for Our Minds
Session Two: The Lure of Knowledge and Power
Session Three: Overcoming Temptation
Session Four: Overcoming Accusation
Session Five: Overcoming Deception
Session Six: Degrees of Spiritual Vulnerability

FIVE

Overcoming Anger

Our Canadian director was conducting a video conference at night and leading people through the Steps to Freedom in Christ during the day. The "pillar" of the church was against having the conference, but he was outvoted, and to everyone's surprise he attended. He was an angry man who ruled through fear and intimidation, but he prided himself as a man of faith whose primary calling was to defend the Bible. Our director asked him to be a prayer partner while he led a young man through the Steps. He agreed. That Wednesday afternoon God set the young man free. That evening the dear old saint asked our director if he would do that for him. "But," he said, "I don't want anyone else in the room." On the final day of the conference he asked the young man, "I was a prayer partner for you; would you be a prayer partner for me?" On Sunday afternoon he finally forgave his father and walked out of the room a free man. His faith had been laced with flesh patterns that kept him in bondage to the past. Can you imagine the damage that was done to his marriage, family, and church?

There is no more important issue to grasp than the nature of faith. Faith is the means by which we live and relate to God. We are saved by faith (see Ephesians 2:8–9), we are sanctified by faith (Ephesians 3:1–5), and we live by faith (2 Corinthians 5:7). "And without faith it is impossible to please God, because anyone who comes to him must believe that he exists and that he rewards those who earnestly seek him" (Hebrews 11:6 NIV1984). What we believe is directly related to how we live and how we emotionally respond to the circumstances of life. There are three basic principles of faith that when understood can keep us on the right path and prevent us from acting presumptuously. First, faith is dependent upon its object. In reality, everyone lives by faith; it is the operating principle of life. The only difference between Christian faith and non-Christian faith is the object of our faith. The issue is not *whether* one believes or doesn't believe. The real issue is *in what* or *in whom* one believes. One cannot have faith in faith!

Hope is the parent of faith. The biblical idea of hope is not wishful thinking. Rather, hope is the present assurance of some future good. People don't proceed by faith if they have no hope. Suppose you want to catch a bus. You walk to the bus stop in faith, hoping the bus will be on time and that the schedule is right. If the bus never comes and the schedule is wrong, your hope is dashed and you lose faith in the public transportation system. If you never had any hope of catching the bus, it would be foolish to proceed by faith. "Now faith is confidence in what we hope for and assurance about what we do not see" (Hebrews 11:1 NIV2011).

God and His Word are the only legitimate objects of our faith, because they never change. "Jesus Christ is the same yesterday and today and forever" (Hebrews 13:8). We learn to trust people who are true to their word and trust in things that have proven to be consistent. It takes time to establish trust in something or someone, because the process of building faith requires consistent and continuous behavior demonstrated over time. That is why human relationships are so fragile. It may take months or years to establish a high degree of trust in another person, but one act of unfaithfulness can destroy it. We can choose to forgive those who have betrayed us, but it often takes a long time, if ever, to regain the trust that has been lost.

Second, how much faith we have is dependent upon how well we know the object of our faith. That is why Christian "faith comes by hearing, and hearing by the word of God" (Romans 10:17 NKJV). If we have little knowledge of God and His Word, we can only have a little faith. Stepping out in faith beyond that which we know to be true is presumption. Believing something to be true does not make it true. Jesus is the Truth, and therefore we believe Him; and He would still be the Truth if we didn't believe Him. Truth and reality are not conditioned by our belief. We can't create our own reality and truth by believing harder. That is a New Age concept derived from the original lie that we are gods who need only to be enlightened.

Third, *faith* is an action word. James wrote, "You have faith and I have works; show me your faith without works, and I will show you my faith by my works" (James 2:18). Every action is preceded by a thought. Behavioral objectives can only be accomplished by changing what one believes. Coercing someone to behave without a corresponding inner conviction is the hypocrisy of legalism. People don't always live according to what they profess, but they do live according to what they believe. Of course, we are justified by faith and faith alone. "For you are all sons of God through faith in Christ Jesus" (Galatians 3:26; see also Romans 3:28); however, if what you profess to believe doesn't affect your walk and your talk, then your faith is only a preference that will dissipate under pressure. Biblical faith is not mental assent to God. It is a demonstrated reliance in God.

Goals and Desires

So how does faith or what we believe relate to anger, the subject of this chapter? Flesh patterns are all based on prior beliefs formulated in our minds before we came to Christ. For instance, the "pillar" of the church mentioned earlier learned how to cope and defend himself against his abusive father. He probably consciously or subconsciously held on to his anger as a means of protecting himself against further abuse. Paul's list of flesh patterns in Galatians 5:19–21 includes "outbursts of anger, disputes, dissensions, factions" (v. 20). A major shift in thinking should take place upon conversion. We were heading in one direction based on how we learned to live independently of God. If repentance is genuine, it will precipitate a turning away from our old ways and start living by faith according to what God says is true.

Before Christ, we had preconceived notions about how to live and meet our own needs of acceptance, security, significance, and success. Usually they are based on the worldly standards of appearance, performance, and social status. Take a moment to reflect on how you would complete these statements: "I would be accepted if . . ." "I would be secure if . . ." "I would be significant if . . ." "I would be successful if . . ." However you completed those sentences reveals what you presently believe and how you are right now living accordingly by faith. I believe God wants all His children to feel accepted, secure, and significant and to live a successful life. Surely you don't believe that our loving heavenly Father wants us to feel rejected, insecure, and insignificant and see us fail in our attempts to do "good works, which God prepared beforehand so that we would walk in them" (Ephesians 2:10)! How we define those issues and how we realize them in our experience is the critical question.

Consciously or subconsciously we begin every day with some idea of what we would like to do and accomplish. Suppose your plan for the day is to drive to a job interview scheduled for 10:00 a.m. You leave early, but a traffic accident has turned the road into a parking lot. The accident blocks your goal of getting to the interview on time! How would you feel? You arrive late, and the interview is less than definitive. They say they will get back to you within a week. Now how do you feel, since your goal is uncertain? The potential job would be career-changing and is a critical part of your goal to have a successful career. They choose someone more qualified and subtly suggest that you should consider another career track. Now how do you feel? It is natural to feel angry when plans or goals are blocked, to feel anxious when they are uncertain, and to feel depressed when they seem impossible.

No God-given goal for our lives can be impossible, uncertain, or blocked. Even the secular world knows that the authority of leaders is undermined if they issue commands that cannot be obeyed. So if God wants something done, it can be done! "For nothing will be impossible with God" (Luke 1:37), and "I can do all things through Christ who strengthens me" (Philippians 4:13 NKJV). "All things," however, have to be consistent with God's will.

To understand how we can successfully live the Christian life, we need to make a distinction between godly goals and personal desires. *A godly goal is any specific orientation that reflects God's purpose for our lives and that is not dependent on people or circumstances beyond our right or ability to control.* The only person we have the right and the ability to control is ourselves. Nobody and nothing can keep us from being the person God created us to be, and that is God's goal for our lives. Circumstances should never define who we are, nor should we allow other people to have that kind of power over us. Only God has the right to determine who we are.

Suppose your goal is to have a loving, harmonious, happy Christian marriage and family. Who can block that goal? Every member in the family can block that goal, and since they are something less than perfect, they will. There is no way you can control every member of your family to accomplish your desire. But if you seek God's goal for you—to become the spouse and parent God created you to be—the only one who can block that goal is you.

A godly desire is any specific orientation that depends on the cooperation of other people, the success of events, or favorable circumstances that we have no right or ability to control. We cannot base our identity, success, or sense of worth on our desires, no matter how godly they may be, because we cannot control their fulfillment. God desires that all repent and live (see Ezekiel 18:32), but not all will. God writes to His children so that they may not sin (see 1 John 2:1), but His sovereignty and His success are not dependent on whether or not we sin.

Suppose a well-meaning pastor has a goal to triple the size of his church and win their community to Christ. Although his desire is a worthy one, every member of the community can block that goal. Relentless in his pursuit, the pastor tries to manipulate the flock and pressure them to produce. The church will suffer a lot of pain and conflict until he realizes that God's goal is for him to become the pastor God created him to be, and that pursuing God's goal is the best way to reach his community for Christ. Do you believe that?

The church growth movement did well in emphasizing biblical principles of evangelism, but too many pastors were left feeling like failures when their churches didn't grow. The goal was to be good witnesses and teach others to be as well. If there had been more focus on pastoring and liberating the congregation, church growth would have happened. What kind of witness to our communities do we have if professing Christians are living defeated lives? Frankly, most unbelievers don't want to become like us! Try setting them free from their anger, fear, anxiety, depression, lust, etc., and you will become a disciple-making church. Offer that possibility to your community, and your church will grow.

There is nothing wrong with having godly desires such as reaching our communities for Christ or having loving, harmonious, happy families. However, we shouldn't base our identities and senses of worth on the fulfillment of those desires. We should never try to control and manipulate people in order to accomplish our desires, nor should we get angry, anxious, or depressed if our desires are not met—though we may feel disappointed. Life is full of disappointments, but they are likely God's appointments to greater maturity in Christ. Other people don't always cooperate and events don't always go our way, but these realities of life are not keeping us from conforming to the image of God.

A man shared with me how hearing this truth liberated him. He explained that he was an angry suit salesperson. His unbelieving boss had to pull him aside many times to dispel his anger, which was undermining his witness. To be a successful salesperson and adequate provider at home, he believed that he had to sell a certain amount of suits. After attending one of our conferences, he realized that he had the wrong goal. He decided to become the suit salesperson that God created him to be and to consider the other person more important than himself. He actually talked a man out of buying a suit that wasn't appropriate for him. His boss noticed how much more peaceful he was, and to his own astonishment, the man sold more suits the week following the conference than he ever had before.

The fruit (not fruits) of the Spirit is love (see Galatians 5:22), which is also the goal of our instruction (1 Timothy 1:5) and the character of God (1 John 4:8). Trying to achieve our desires, regardless of how godly they appear, may result in character traits and emotional responses that are in direct contrast to the fruit of the Spirit:

Unfulfilled desires may result in . . .	instead of godly goals that result in love:
Anger	Joy
Anxiety	Peace
Depression	Patience (Long-suffering)
Harshness	Kindness
Meanness	Goodness
Faithlessness	Faithfulness
Forcefulness	Gentleness
Controlling	Self-control

If a lot of our desires (even godly ones) aren't realized, then what is the basis for our hope? Paul answers in Romans 5:3–5,

> We also exult in our tribulations, knowing that tribulation brings about perseverance; and perseverance, proven character; and proven character, hope; and hope does not disappoint, because the love of God has been poured out within our hearts through the Holy Spirit who was given to us.

Many trials and tribulations reveal wrong goals but also actually make possible God's goal for our lives, which is proven character. The very thing we hope for is realized when we live by faith according to what God says is true.

Having the wrong goal may lead to faulty conclusions: "This job is hopeless; therefore, I should change jobs." "This church is hopeless; therefore, I should change churches." "This marriage is hopeless; therefore, I should leave this marriage." There may be legitimate times to change churches and jobs, but lessons unlearned will carry over to the next location. A hopeless marriage will remain such until we decide to be the spouse God created us to be and stop trying to change the other person. How much anger exhibited in our churches and homes would dissipate if we were all filled with the Holy Spirit and were committed to God's goal (will) for our lives, which is our sanctification (see 1 Thessalonians 4:3).

There is another side to anger that is justified, and that is righteous indignation. If we wish to be angry and not sin, then be angry like Jesus was and be angry at sin. He turned over the tables in the temple, not the money changers. God has no blocked, uncertain, or impossible goals. He doesn't get angry, yet the Bible refers often to the wrath of God. I believe that righteous indignation is part of God's unchanging nature, and I think it should be part of ours—otherwise we would never seek to right those things that are wrong. We are called to be salt and light in a fallen world, but our awareness of what is sinful can easily grow dull with tolerance and exposure to it. The profanity and explicit sex commonly accepted today in television and movies would never have been tolerated fifty years ago. Alexander Pope said it well:

> Vice is a monster of so frightful mein,
> As to be hated needs but to be seen;
> Yet seen too oft, familiar with her face,
> We first endure, then pity, then embrace.[1]

Learning to manage our anger when life doesn't go our way is part of our maturation process. Anger itself is not the problem. It is a God-given emotion signaling that something is wrong. So "be angry, and yet do not sin; do not let the sun go down on your anger, and do not give the devil an opportunity [literally a place]" (Ephesians 4:26–27). As soon as anger surfaces, separate what is a goal and what is a desire in your mind. For example, imagine you're in traffic; the light has changed, but the car in front of you doesn't budge. Of course you desire to get through that intersection, but you are still a child of God, and such moments provide you the opportunity to live like one.

You have the God-given capacity to choose what you think and believe. You don't control your anger; you control your thoughts—by taking every thought captive to the obedience of Christ. If the anger is righteous, God may be directing you to pray for someone or motivating you to right some wrong. Paul is telling us to analyze the cause for our anger and deal with the aftermath before the sun sets, or we may be giving the devil grounds for harassment. It is double jeopardy if the devil gave us the thought that made us angry. We can manage our emotions today by monitoring what we think and believe, but what about the emotional baggage we carry from our past?

Healing Wounds and Setting Captives Free

When I taught pastoral counseling at Talbot School of Theology, I started the class by having them sit in triads. They would individually respond to a series of questions and then rotate to other groups. For many it was a positive experience, but for some it was threatening. When asked to describe their home experience between the ages of six and twelve, a student asked, "Why are you making us do this?" She was an adult child of an alcoholic, and all her memories of that time in her life were painful. Another student came to see me the next day. He also found the exercise difficult, which indicates something in his past is still affecting him today.

If I were to talk with a group of Christians about rape, the intensity of emotional response would range from two to ten. It would be near two for those who have never been raped and don't know anybody who has been raped. It would be from three to eight for those who know someone who has been raped.

But the emotional response would be near ten for someone who has been raped. Have you ever had a conversation with a group of Christians about something potentially controversial, and suddenly someone responds angrily and leaves? You probably wondered, *What did I say?* Your words or attitude triggered a painful memory. Almost everyone has "hot buttons" from the past that are triggered by present events. When I was a seminary student, a fellow student apologized for being standoffish toward me. It hadn't gone unnoticed by me, and I was wondering if I had somehow offended him. It turned out that I resembled his high school wrestling coach, whom he despised.

People have a tendency to avoid people, conversations, or events that trigger painful memories. *I'm not going there if he or she is going to be there. I stay away from movies like that. If you are going to talk about that subject, I'm leaving.* If you have had enough pain in the past, your world can start shutting down. Time doesn't heal old wounds, and if they are never dealt with, people will bounce off each other's wounds for the rest of their lives.

We can try to suppress those painful memories by attempting to manage our thoughts and avoiding certain people and events, but that will only keep us bound to the past. There is one primary truth and one choice that can set us free. First, as new believers, we are not just products of our pasts. We are new creations in Christ. God doesn't fix our past. He sets us free from it. We processed every experience in our past at the time it happened. Remember, we are not in bondage to past events, but we may be in bondage to the lies we believe as a result of our past experiences. As new creations in Christ, we can reprocess those events from the perspective of a conqueror in Christ, not as a victim. I cannot promise anyone that they won't be victimized, but I can promise them that they don't have to remain victims anymore.

A missionary couple had recently returned from a long stay overseas, but before the wife went back to see her natural family, she attended my one-week summer intensive class, Resolving Personal and Spiritual Conflicts. She wrote me a letter sharing her newfound freedom. Then she went home to her very dysfunctional family and discovered that her father was carrying on a homosexual affair. After the visit, she made an appointment to see me. She wondered what she should do about it—she wasn't certain if her mother knew about the affair and was concerned her father might have AIDS or some other sexually transmitted disease.

I said, "Let's put this in perspective. Aren't you glad that you found out about your father after the conference this summer?" She said, "If I had gone straight home to that mess, I think I would have had a total breakdown." Then I asked, "Knowing this about your father, what does that do to your heritage?" She started to answer, but then a smile broke out on her face and she said, "Nothing. I'm a child of God."

Second, if we want to experience our freedom from the past, we must choose to forgive those who have offended us. Angry people will stay that way until they forgive those who have offended them. It is inevitable that we will suffer at the hands of others, no matter how righteously we live. Physical and emotional abuse can leave us feeling bitter, angry, and resentful. Our old nature seeks revenge and repayment, but the Spirit says, "Forgive them, just as Christ has forgiven you" (see Colossians 3:13). "But you don't know how badly they have hurt me!" As long as we hold on to our bitterness, they are still hurting us. Forgiveness sets us free from our past and stops the pain. We don't heal in order to forgive; we forgive in order to heal.

Forgiveness is not forgetting. God says, "I will forgive their wickedness and will remember their sins no more" (Hebrews 8:12 NIV1984). That doesn't mean God forgets, because an omniscient God couldn't forget even if He wanted to. It means that He will not use our past sins against us in the future. He will remove them as far from us as the east is from the west (see Psalm 103:12). We know that we haven't forgiven others if we continuously bring up the past and use it against them. Forgetting may be a long-term by-product of forgiving, but it is not the means by which we forgive. Nor are we tolerating sin when we forgive others. God forgives, but He never tolerates sin. We have the right to set up scriptural boundaries to stop future abuse.

Jesus forgave us by taking upon himself the consequences of our sin. To forgive others as Christ has forgiven us means that we agree to live with the consequences of their sin. That may not seem fair, but we will have to do it anyway. Everyone is living with the consequences of someone else's sin. We are all living with the consequence of Adam's sin. The only real choice is whether we will do so in the bondage of bitterness or in the freedom of forgiveness.

As long as we refuse to forgive, we are emotionally chained to past events and the people who hurt us. The purpose of forgiveness is to set the captive free and then realize we have been the captives. Bitterness is like swallowing poison and hoping the other person will die. It is for our own benefit that we forgive others.

But where is the justice? The cross is what makes forgiveness morally correct. Christ died once for *all* our sins. His sins, her sins, my sins, and your sins. There has always been an elevation of social justice whenever Christianity flourished. However, we will never have perfect justice in this lifetime, which is why there is a coming final judgment. The old nature wants revenge, but God said, "Do not take revenge, my friends, but leave room for God's wrath, for it is written: 'It is mine to avenge; I will repay,' says the Lord" (Romans 12:19 NIV 1984). But why should we let them off the hook? That is precisely why we should forgive—because we are still hooked to them. If we let them off our hook, are they off God's hook? What is to be gained in forgiving others is freedom from our past. We have to believe that God will exact justice in the final judgment.

Forgiving others doesn't mean refusing to testify in civil courts for the sake of social justice. Nor does it mean we avoid confronting a brother or sister who is living in sin. Forgiving others makes our heart right before God and allows us to experience our freedom in Christ. Only then can we righteously testify in court and confront others. If you have offended someone, don't attempt to worship God when you come under conviction (see Matthew 5:24). Go first to the person who has something against you, seek forgiveness, pay for damages if necessary, and be reconciled. If someone has offended you, don't go to that person. Go first to God and forgive that person as Christ has forgiven you.

Many people wrongly think they have to go to the people who offended them in order to forgive them. That may be impossible and often is inadvisable. The person we need to forgive may be dead or unreachable. In some cases it would be unwise, because confronting an offender who is unrepentant may actually set a person up for more abuse.

Jesus says we should continue forgiving as many times as necessary (see Matthew 18:22), and then He tells the parable of the unmerciful servant to put our need to forgive others in perspective. "Ten thousand talents," the amount the servant owed the king (v. 24), was way beyond a lifetime wage. Repaying the debt was not possible for the servant; therefore, he had no choice but to throw himself on his master's mercy. In comparison, the "hundred denarii" this man demanded from his fellow servant (v. 28) was equal to just a few months' wages. His master had forgiven him an enormous debt, but the man showed no mercy to his fellow servant.

God is just and can't be unjust or unrighteous for a moment. Justice is rightness or fairness. If we meted out justice, we would be giving people what they deserve. We would all be consigned to hell if God gave us what we deserved. Thankfully, God is also merciful, and mercy is not giving people what they deserve. If we throw ourselves upon the mercy of the court, we are admitting to our guilt and asking for something less than what we deserve. Grace is giving to others what they don't deserve. What we have freely received we are to extend to others. We are to forgive as we have been forgiven. We are to be merciful to others as God has been merciful to us. In other words, don't give others what they deserve, but don't stop there. Give them what they don't deserve. Love one another.

How do you forgive others from your heart? In the Steps to Freedom in Christ, we start by asking the Lord to reveal to our minds the people we need to forgive, including all those we have negative feelings toward. Don't overlook the need to let yourself off your own hook. Many have said that forgiving themselves was the hardest one on the list. God had already forgiven them, and there is no condemnation for those who are in Christ Jesus. In essence they are just accepting God's forgiveness, but I have found it very helpful for them to specifically say, "I forgive myself for [whatever they have done]." In many cases I have discovered that they are being victimized by the accuser who "accuses them before our God day and night" (Revelation 12:10).

Second, face the hurt and the feelings of hatred. If you are going to forgive from the heart, you have to allow the painful memories to surface. If you are unwilling to admit to the pain and the emotional damage, the forgiveness process will be incomplete. Humanly we try to suppress our emotional pain, but God will surface names and events so we can face them and let them go. To admit that you hate your parents, for instance, only means that you can now forgive them. Your feelings toward others will change after you forgive them. What is to be gained is your freedom.

One woman was working through her list and asked for a break to visit the restroom. She had dealt with only ten offenders up to that point, and just one of those abusers would send an average person into a tailspin. When she came back and looked at the list, she asked, "Why do the names on the top of the list look different to me than the remaining names?" Before forgiveness she couldn't mention those names without triggering painful memories. They no longer had any hold on her. That is what freedom brings.

Third, forgiveness is a crisis of the will. You choose to bear the consequences of the person's sin. You choose to let go of the past and grab hold of God. You choose not to seek revenge. Don't wait until you feel like forgiving, because you will never get there. God is not asking you to like the person who offended you; He is asking you to forgive as you have been forgiven so that He can set you free and heal your damaged emotions. Let Him be the avenger. Stop the pain by forgiving from your heart every person who has offended you for every offensive thing he or she did. You can do this by praying (preferably out loud), "Lord, I forgive [person] for [verbally express every hurt and pain the Lord brings to your mind and how it made you feel]."

Fourth, after you have forgiven every person for every painful memory, finish by praying, "Lord, I release all these people to you, and I release my right to seek revenge. I choose not to hold on to my bitterness and anger, and I ask you to heal my damaged emotions. In Jesus' name, I pray. Amen."

After many years of leading thousands through the Steps to Freedom in Christ, I can say without qualification that forgiving others is the biggest issue confronting believers. The average person will have twenty to thirty names surface when they pray.

Forgiving another person from our hearts is the most Christlike decision we will ever make. Several years ago I was speaking to six hundred Christian leaders. I asked them, "How many here have given a message Sunday morning on what it means to forgive others from our hearts and explained how to do it, or have heard such a message?" Not one person raised a hand.

Our basic discipleship course has an entire lesson on forgiveness. When I taught it as a conference, I prayed, asking God on behalf of all those who attended to bring to our minds those people we needed to forgive. I waited a couple of minutes and then said, "I am not going to embarrass anyone, but I sense the need to give you an opportunity to respond to God. If you know there is one or more persons you need to forgive, and you are willing to do that, would you stand right now. I will not ask for anything more than that, but in standing you are saying, 'God, I hear you, and I am willing to forgive, and I need your grace to do that.'" I have never seen less than 95 percent stand.

During the Steps, inquirers pray, asking the Lord to reveal to their minds whom they need to forgive. When the list is complete, I ask, "If you forgave these people, what would you be doing?" Nobody to this day has given me anywhere near a right answer. If our ministry is reconciliation, and if we want to be a disciple-making church, then we have to teach our people how to forgive others and give them regular opportunities to do so.

SIX

Overcoming Anxiety Disorders

Dr. Edmund Bourne is the author of *The Anxiety and Phobia Workbook*,[1] which won the Benjamin Franklin Award for excellence in psychology. Dr. Bourne entered this field of study because he personally struggled with anxiety. Five years after the publication of the first edition, his own anxiety disorder took a turn for the worse. This caused him to reevaluate his own life as well as his approach to treatment. In 1998 he published *Healing Fear*. In the introduction he wrote:

> The guiding metaphor for this book is "healing," as an approach to overcoming anxiety, in contrast to "applied technology." I feel it's important to introduce this perspective into the field of anxiety treatment since the vast majority of self-help books available (including my first book) utilize the applied technology approach. . . . I don't want to diminish the importance of cognitive behavioral therapy (CBT) and the applied technology approach. Such an approach produces effective results in many cases, and I use it in my professional practice every day. In the

past few years, though, I feel that the cognitive behavioral strategy has reached its limits. CBT and medication can produce results quickly and are very compatible with the brief therapy, managed-care environment in the mental health profession at present. When follow-up is done over one- to three-year intervals, however, some of the gains are lost. Relapses occur rather often, and people seem to get themselves back into the same difficulties that precipitated the original anxiety disorder.[2]

In other words, "They have healed the brokenness of My people superficially, saying, 'Peace, peace,' but there is no peace" (Jeremiah 6:14). Before we get too smug about our successes of applying the gospel with "effective results," we too must acknowledge that many will fall back to their old flesh patterns unless they genuinely repent. I mentioned earlier that cognitive behavior therapy (CBT) is compatible with repentance, but it will fall far short if the process does not include God and if it overlooks the reality of the spiritual world. I don't know whether Dr. Bourne has a saving knowledge of the Lord Jesus Christ, but in his own research he came to the following conclusion: "In my own experience, spirituality has been important, and I believe it will come to play an increasingly important role in the psychology of the future."[3] I hope he is right, but I predict that any new emphasis on spirituality will not necessarily be Christian. The number one spokesperson in America for psychosomatic illness at present is Dr. Deepak Chopra, who espouses Hinduism. I mentioned his name to my doctor, and she said, "Oh, isn't he wonderful!" She was surprised when I said, "No, he isn't!" I asked her if any medicine would be appropriate for anybody as long as the food and drug administration approved it. "Of course not," she said. "So any spirituality is okay?" I asked.

Anxiety disorders include fear, anxiety, and panic attacks. Fear is the most basic instinct of every living creature. An animal without fear will become some predator's dinner. Fear is a God-given natural response to anything that threatens our physical safety and psychological well-being. Rational fears are learned and vital for our survival. Falling off a chair at an early age develops a healthy respect for heights. Touching a hot stove teaches us to stay away from other items that will burn us. Phobias are irrational fears that compel us to do irresponsible things or inhibit us from doing what we should. The key to overcoming any phobia is to identify the lie behind its irrationality, which is another confirmation that truth sets us free.

Fear is different from anxiety and panic attacks, because fear has an object. Fears or phobias are categorized by their objects. Acrophobia is a fear of high places. Claustrophobia is a fear of enclosed places. Agoraphobia is a generalized fear of public settings (*agora* is the Greek word for "marketplace"). Toxophobia is a fear of being poisoned. And so on. In order for a fear object to be effective, it must be perceived by humans or animals as having two attributes. It must be imminent (present) and potent (possessing some power that can negatively affect us).

I believe that I have a reasonably healthy fear of rattlesnakes. However, I have no fear of them as I sit writing this chapter, because there are none present. If one slithered through the door and coiled under my chair unnoticed by me, I would still sense no fear, because I would have no awareness of its presence. However, my fear index would go from zero to ten immediately upon seeing it at my feet. If you threw a dead rattlesnake at my feet (provided I was sure that it was dead), I wouldn't fear it. Remove just one of those attributes—its imminence or its potency—and the fear dissipates.

It is important to recognize the learned aspect of fear objects. Suppose a two-year-old child playing in your backyard sees a harmless garden snake slithering along in the grass. The child will likely pick it up, but the average mother will probably freak out. Another adult who knows that the snake is harmless will have little fear of the snake. Total ignorance is dangerous, partial knowledge can be paralyzing, but complete knowledge liberates. Most fears are subsets of three major fear objects—namely, death, people, and Satan. For instance, the fear of death is the likely root of claustrophobia (suffocating to death) and acrophobia (dying from a fall). We can overcome all irrational fears by knowing the truth, and by knowing that God has removed one of the attributes for the three major fear objects.

Physical death is imminent "inasmuch as it is appointed for men to die once and after this comes judgment" (Hebrews 9:27), but it is no longer potent, because of the resurrection of Jesus. "'Death is swallowed up in victory. O death, where is your victory? O death, where is your sting?'" (1 Corinthians 15:54–55). Jesus said, "I am the resurrection and the life; he who believes in Me will live [spiritually] even if he dies [physically], and everyone who lives and believes in Me will never die [spiritually]" (John 11:25–26). Every born-again believer can say with Paul, "For to me, to live is Christ and to die is gain" (Philippians 1:21). Many people believe that dying is the worst thing that can happen to them, but Paul says otherwise. Absence from the body is to be present with the Lord in a resurrected body that has no pain. The ultimate value is being in union with God, not with our body, which someday we will all separate from. Jim Elliot, the martyred missionary, wrote, "He is no fool who gives up that which he cannot keep in order to gain what he cannot lose."[4] Knowing this truth is not a license to commit suicide, because we are supposed to be good stewards of the physical life God has entrusted to us. The person who is free from the fear of death is free to live today.

Phobias rooted in the fear of people include rejection, failure, abandonment, and even death. Jesus said, "Do not fear those who kill the body but are unable to kill the soul; but rather fear

Him who is able to destroy both soul and body in hell" (Matthew 10:28). Peter wrote, "Do not fear their intimidation, and do not be troubled, but sanctify Christ as Lord in your hearts, always being ready to make a defense to everyone who asks you to give an account for the hope that is in you, yet with gentleness and reverence" (1 Peter 3:14–15). The number one reason Christians don't share their faith is the fear of people or, more specifically, the fear of rejection and failure. Is it rational that we should let those fears keep others from hearing the good news?

Why is the fear of God the beginning of wisdom (see Proverbs 9:10)? How can that fear overcome all other fears? God is the ultimate fear object because He is omnipresent (imminent) and omnipotent. When we worship God, we are ascribing to Him His divine attributes. The Father seeks those who do that in spirit and in truth (see John 4:23). That is not because He needs us to tell Him who He is. It is for our benefit that we worship God in order to keep His divine attributes fresh in our minds. Isaiah wrote:

> You are not to say, "It is a conspiracy!" In regard to all that this people call a conspiracy, and you are not to fear what they fear or be in dread of it. "It is the Lord of hosts whom you should regard as holy. And He shall be your fear, and He shall be your dread. Then He shall become a sanctuary."
>
> Isaiah 8:12–14

Spirit-filled Christians who know the truth have found their sanctuary in Christ. They are the true worshipers that God is seeking.

God rules supreme over every other fear object—including Satan. Even though "your adversary, the devil, prowls about like a roaring lion, seeking someone to devour" (1 Peter 5:8), he has been defeated (imminent, but not potent). Jesus came for the purpose of destroying the works of the devil (see 1 John 3:8). "When He had disarmed the rulers and authorities, He made a public display of them, having triumphed over them through Him" (Colossians 2:15). Most people in your church fear Satan more than they fear God. In doing so they elevate Satan as a greater object of worship.

Fear of Failure

While teaching a doctor of ministry class, I had all the pastors complete this statement: "The thing I fear the most is . . ." Each stated it differently, but fear of failure was the essence of every response. None said *God*. I have been surprised to learn that the fear of failure is a universal problem plaguing many people. Trying not to fail distracts us from succeeding without being driven. Allowing any fear object other than God to control us prevents or hinders us from living by faith in God. I believe there are three principles of success that are not dependent upon other people or circumstances.

First, to be successful we need to know God and His ways. The Israelites had been liberated from Egypt, but they were about to face some giants in the Promised Land. Joshua wrote, "Only be strong and very courageous; be careful to do according to all the law which Moses My servant commanded you; do not turn from it to the right or to the left, so that you may have success wherever you go" (Joshua 1:7). Paul wrote, "I count all things to be loss in view of the surpassing value of knowing Christ Jesus my Lord" (Philippians 3:8).

Second, to be successful we must strive to become the person God has called us to be (see Philippians 3:12–14). We would have many more successful Christians if we put character before career, maturity before ministry, and being before doing.

Third, to be successful we must be good stewards of the time, talent, and treasure God has entrusted us with (see 1 Corinthians 4:1–2).

No fear of any person should keep us from following those three principles. We have to start playing for the Coach and stop playing for the grandstand.

Just as important as knowing what constitutes success is knowing what failure is not. To stumble and fall is not failure. "For a righteous man falls seven times, and rises again" (Proverbs 24:16). To stumble and fall again is not failure. Failure comes when you say, "I was pushed." A mistake is never a failure, unless you fail to learn from it. A young executive was about to replace a highly successful chief executive officer. He asked the CEO, "Sir, how do you account for your incredible success." The CEO sternly said, "No mistakes." "But, sir," replied the young man, "how do you get to the point where you make no mistakes? "A lot of experience," was the reply. "What kind of experience do you mean?" "A lot of mistakes."

Overcoming Irrational Fears

Overcoming any conflicts begins by reconciling with God. David wrote, "I sought the Lord, and He answered me, and delivered me from all my fears. . . . The angel of the Lord encamps around those who fear Him, and rescues them" (Psalm 34:4, 7). That is why I always start with the Steps to Freedom in Christ. The research shared in chapter 3 reveals that much resolution of many fears comes by resolving personal and spiritual conflicts— i.e., by seeking first the kingdom of God, as illustrated by the following testimony:

> For the past thirty-five years, I have lived from one surge of adrenaline to the next. My entire life has been gripped by

paralyzing fears, which seem to come from nowhere and everywhere—fears that made very little sense to me or anyone else. I invested four years of my life obtaining a degree in psychology, hoping it would enable me to understand and conquer those fears. Psychology only perpetuated my questions and insecurity. Six years of professional counseling offered little insight and no change in my level of anxiety.

After two hospitalizations, trips to the emergency room, repeated EKGs, a visit to the thoracic surgeon, and a battery of other tests, my panic attacks only worsened. By the time I came to see you, full-blown panic attacks had become a daily feature.

It has been three weeks since I've experienced a panic attack! I have gone to the malls and church services. I have played for an entire worship service, and even made it through Sunday school with peace in my heart. I had no idea what freedom meant until now. When I came to see you, I had hoped that the truth would set me free, but now I know it has. . . .

I could barely read a verse of Scripture at one sitting. It was as though someone snatched it away from my mind as soon as it entered. Scripture was such a fog to me. I could only hear the verses that spoke of death and punishment. I had actually become afraid to open my Bible. These past three weeks I have spent hours a day in the Word, and it makes sense. The fog is gone.

Not all fears are overcome that easily, because flesh patterns remain, and that which has been learned must now be unlearned. I offer the following steps to overcome irrational fears:

First, start by analyzing your fears. What are you afraid of? What event precipitated your first experience of that fear? There is always a cause and an effect. Ask God to reveal that to you. What is the root lie that makes the fear irrational? Which attribute of the fear object can be eliminated?

Second, analyze your lifestyle. Fear is a powerful motivator for good and evil. How has that fear prevented you from living a responsible life, compelled you to do that which is irresponsible, or led you to compromise your witness? A timid Christian home-maker who fears her pagan husband will likely compromise her witness, leading to irresponsible behavior. An intimidated employee may lie for his or her boss even though he or she knows it is wrong. Students may succumb to peer pressure and compromise their faith because they are afraid their friends will reject them.

Third, decide on a responsible plan of action. So far you have submitted to God and resisted the devil, and identified your fears and the lies behind them. And you understand how the fear is negatively affecting your behavior. The next step is to face the fear and prayerfully work out a realistic plan to overcome it. If you are afraid to ride an elevator, choose a two-story building where you can enter the elevator and come out before the door closes. Then open the door and let it close on you. Then open it again. Finally, go in and push the button for the second floor. Have a friend ride with you if necessary. Don't start by going to the Empire State Building and pushing the button for the top floor. The ministry Evangelism Explosion was successful because it helped trainees overcome their fears by going with an experienced trainer and observing. Then they were encouraged to participate with the trainer, and the final step was to take the lead while the trainer observed.

Fourth, if the fear object is a person, determine in advance how you will respond to his or her possible reactions to your plan. How should you respond if the person ignores you, gets mad at you, or threatens harm when you no longer let him or her control your life?

Fifth, commit yourself to carry out the plan in the power of the Holy Spirit. Do the thing you fear the most, and the death of that fear is certain. There is no other way to overcome fearful flesh patterns. We want the fear to go away so we can live responsibly, but it is the other way around.

Anxiety

Anxiety is like fear without an adequate cause. People are anxious because they don't know what is going to happen next. The word *anxiety* occurs about twenty-five times in the New Testament. It sometimes is used in the positive sense of caring. People are deemed mentally healthy if they are *relatively* free from anxiety. If you have an important exam tomorrow, you should feel anxious. The proper response is to study. If your teenager is two hours late getting home, you should feel anxious. Your first response should be prayer.

Jesus confronts anxiety in the Sermon on the Mount by questioning what we treasure and in whom we trust. "Do not store up for yourselves treasures on earth, where moth and rust destroy, and where thieves break in and steal. But store up treasures in heaven" (Matthew 6:19–20). Treasures on earth have two characteristics. First, according to the law of entropy, all systems become increasingly disorderly and eventually decay; therefore, constant concern is necessary to maintain all our earthly treasures. Second, there will always be thieves who covet what others have; therefore, security for our possessions is necessary. It is hard to be anxiety-free while worrying about our possessions, which we can't take with us. Storing up treasures in heaven is profitable for this age and the one to come. "For where your treasure is, there your heart will be also" (v. 21). Anxious people love things and use people. Peacemakers use things to love people. Peaceful existence and a sense of security come from meaningful relationships, not material possessions.

Jesus continues, "The eye is the lamp of the body; so then if the eye is clear, your whole body will be full of light. But if your eye is bad, your whole body will be full of darkness" (vv. 22–23). Ancient tradition viewed the eyes as the window through which light entered the body. If the eyes were in good condition, the whole body would receive the benefits that light bestows. If bad, the whole body would be plunged into darkness, which breeds disease. There is a subtle nuance in this passage that is pregnant with meaning. The "clear eye" is the one with a single vision, which Jesus clarifies in the next verse: "No one can serve two masters; for either he will hate the one and love the other, or he will be devoted to one and despise the other. You cannot serve God and wealth" (v. 24).

Anxiety (*merimna* in the Greek) is a combination of *merizo*, which means "divide," and *nous*, which means "mind." In other words, an anxious person is double-minded, and according to James, a double-minded person is unstable in all their ways (see James 1:8). The King James translation picks up that idea in Matthew 6:25: "Therefore I say unto you, take no thought ("do not be worried about" NASB) for your life." Jesus is saying, "Trust me. I take care of the birds in the air and the lilies of the field, and you are worth far more to me than animals and plants. I know you need food, clothing, and shelter. If you seek first the kingdom of God and His righteousness, all these things will be added to you."

Casting Your Anxiety Upon Christ

First, turn to God in prayer. Paul wrote, "Be anxious for nothing, but in everything by prayer and supplication with thanksgiving let your requests be made known to God" (Philippians 4:6). The first thing a Christian should do about anything is pray.

Second, resolve all personal and spiritual conflicts. I know I am sounding redundant, but I firmly believe the answer lies in drawing closer to God and resisting the devil. If you have thoroughly gone through the Steps to Freedom in Christ, there is no need to keep resolving the same old issue. I regularly lead someone through the Steps to stay in touch with hurting humanity, but I also get a housecleaning every time I do it. Consider the context for Peter's instruction to cast our anxiety on Christ.

> Therefore, humble yourselves under the mighty hand of God, that He may exalt you at the proper time, casting all your anxiety on Him, because He cares for you. Be of sober spirit, be on the alert. Your adversary, the devil, prowls around like a roaring lion, seeking someone to devour. But resist him, firm in your faith.
>
> 1 Peter 5:6–9

If a believer is paying attention to a deceiving spirit, they are double-minded, and therefore anxious.

Third, state the problem. In anxious states of mind, people can't see the forest for the trees. Many anxious people find relief by simply having their problem clarified and put in perspective. A problem well stated is half-solved. Generally speaking, the process of worrying takes a greater toll on a person than the negative consequences of what they worried about. Many are actually relieved when the worst-case scenario actually happens. The danger at this juncture is to seek ungodly counsel or bogus remedies from charlatans and shamans. Peddling temporary cures—such as happy hour and pep pills—for anxiety is a lucrative market, but the peddlers don't care for the person like Jesus does.

Fourth, divide the facts from the assumptions. People may be fearful of the facts, but they are not necessarily anxious. Anxious people don't know what is going to happen tomorrow. Since they don't know, they make assumptions, and human nature usually is to assume the worst. If the assumption is not based on truth, then what one feels is not based on reality.

Fifth, determine what you have the right and ability to control. You are only responsible for what you have the right and ability to control. You are not responsible for that which you don't. Your sense of worth is only tied to that for which you are responsible. If you are living an irresponsible life, you should feel anxious. Don't try to cast your responsibility onto Christ. He will throw it back. But do cast your anxiety onto Him, because His integrity is at stake in meeting your needs if you are living a responsible and righteous life.

Sixth, list everything you can do that is related to the situation that is your responsibility. Then commit yourself to be a responsible person and fulfill your calling and obligations in life. You have done the best you could, and that is all God is asking. Any residual anxiety is probably due to your assuming responsibilities that God never intended you to have.

Panic Attacks

Panic attacks (sometimes referred to as anxiety attacks) are defined as "very frightening and aversive experiences in which people are overwhelmed with the physical symptoms of anxiety."[5] About 75 percent of panic disorder sufferers are women. It usually has its onset between the ages of twenty and thirty, although it can begin in the teenage years or with adults over forty.

After suffering a number of panic episodes, many become increasingly afraid that they are helpless victims of panic. There are approximately one to two million Americans who have pure panic attacks, and that condition will eventually develop into agoraphobia for about a third of them, claiming millions of victims. Since they don't know when an attack may happen, they become fearful of going to public events where such an episode would be highly embarrassing. If they manage to attend church, they will likely sit near an exit.

There is no physical enemy to fight or flee from during a panic attack, yet the body responds as though there is. Symptoms include terror that is almost paralyzing, a racing heartbeat, nausea, lightheadedness, chest pains, sudden chills, and difficulty breathing—feeling as though you can't get enough air. In a real emergency our breathing undergoes a significant change in rate and pattern, which also happens during a panic attack. The initial physical response to a real or imagined fear object is to gasp or suck in air. Then, instead of exhaling, we try to suck in more air, but there is no room for it in the lungs. Having people blow into a paper bag gets them to exhale and return to normal breathing. Knowing that most of the unpleasant physical symptoms of panic attacks are the body's God-created means of coping with a perceived emergency takes a lot of the terrifying mystery out of these episodes. What initially seems to be an overwhelming situation becomes much more manageable if we understand what our bodies naturally do.

Suppose you have a minor condition of mitral valve prolapse, which is usually a non-life-threatening heart palpitation. Your first experience could be frightening, because you don't know what it is and it may seem like a heart attack. After a thorough physical exam you learn that it is only a minor condition. The next time your heart flutters, your renewed mind interprets the data differently and there is no (or less) panic. The first episode would be less frightening if your mind had previously been programmed not to fear death. There are other physical conditions that may result in panic attacks, so a thorough physical exam should always be considered an option for treatment.

There are spiritual mysteries surrounding panic attacks that medicine and secular psychology cannot address. What causes a person who is normally able to handle stress suddenly become stricken with a panic attack? Why do they call it an anxiety attack when it feels much more like fear? Is it because they cannot identify the fear object, therefore it better fits the definition of anxiety? Why do people suddenly awaken terrorized from a sound sleep? Why do Christians often find instantaneous freedom from these attacks when they call upon the name of the Lord? These questions were likely on the mind of someone who contacted our ministry:

I am wondering if you can help me out with a particular experience that has plagued me and my sleep for the past six or seven years. Although I am a Christian, I have probably experienced about fifteen of these panic attacks over the past several years. They are usually associated with a time in which I've given something over to God or committed my ways to His.

Here is a little history about my sleeping habits. When I was young, I would dream very intense dreams about spirits or things related to the spiritual world. I'm not sure why except that I am an artist and have always had a very vivid imagination. Other nights I would dream about the end times and things that happened—very intense dreams also!

As I got older, these dreams would happen less frequently, but when they did come, they came with the same intensity. When I turned seventeen, I received a calling from God—a very distinct one. Unfortunately, because of my pride and fear, I did not follow that calling. Through the years since then I have received many opportunities to follow that original calling, and each time I tried, the panic attack would result. Consequently, I would back off from the calling because of the fear of another attack.

The panic attack usually started by waking me out of my sleep to either a rushing sound in my ear, many people talking incoherently, or many people screaming. By the time this ends (usually in about five or ten seconds), an intense, indescribable, mammoth fear envelops my whole body.

I really can't describe how intense this fear is. My body becomes physically paralyzed, no movement. I can't talk. I can move my eyes around and hear, though. Finally, a heavy weight seems to rest on my chest and pushes me into my bed. At least that is what it feels like. This whole experience lasts about a minute, but then I am usually wide awake and scared. I'm not sure what causes this, but I think it may be demonic.

The fact that the attacks occurred at the time she was making serious moves toward God clearly indicates a spiritual attack. Unfortunately, the scare tactic worked. The fear of something other than God kept her from following Him. This is a very common strategy of Satan. The kind of attack she described would happen to me every night before I began a Resolving Personal and Spiritual Conflicts conference, and it continued for four years. I learned how to stand against such an attack and would fall back to sleep within minutes.

I have asked conference attendees two questions. First, "How many have been sharply awakened at a precise time, namely 3:00 a.m.?" At least a third of the people raised their hands. The people that I have helped come out of Satanism have all reported that 3:00 a.m. is the culmination of their Satanic rituals. I have heard from them and others that Satanists pray for our demise, and attempt to summon and send demons to attack us. It is no sin to be under attack, and believers should know, "You are from God, little children, and have overcome them; because greater is He who is in you than he who is in the world" (1 John 4:4). It is only an annoyance for a person of faith.

Second, "How many have been suddenly overwhelmed with fear at night? You probably felt half-asleep and half-awake. It could feel as though something was pushing on your chest or grabbing your throat. You tried to move or say something, but you couldn't." Again, at least a third of the people raised their hands. When I conducted a conference for 250 leaders of a very high-profile church, 95 percent raised their hands. If we call upon the name of the Lord, we shall be saved, but what if we can't physically do that?

The natural response to fear is to say or do something immediately, but under such attacks it seems as though you can't. It is not a physical fear object, and it can't be resolved physically. "For though we live in the world, we do not wage war as the world does. The weapons we fight with are not the weapons of the world. On the contrary, they have divine power to demolish strongholds" (2 Corinthians 10:3–4 NIV2011). God knows the thoughts and intentions of our heart, so we can always call upon the Lord in our minds. The moment we do, we will be able to speak. All we have to say is "Jesus," and the devil will flee. It needs to be said aloud, because Satan is under no obligation to obey our thoughts, which he doesn't perfectly know. The order of Scripture is critical. We must first submit to God inwardly, and then we will be able to resist the devil outwardly (see James 4:7).

Spiritual attacks usually occur at night when we are alone and more vulnerable. Being awakened out of a sound sleep heightens our sense of terror, as we are caught off guard and easily confused. There are many references in Scripture where humans are overwhelmed with fear in the presence of angelic beings. Job's friend Eliphaz described an experience he had:

> "Now a word was brought to me stealthily, and my ear received a whisper of it. Amid disquieting thoughts from the visions of the night, when deep sleep falls on men, dread came upon me, and trembling, and made all my bones shake. Then a spirit passed by my face; the hair of my flesh bristled up. It stood still, but I could not discern its appearance; a form was before my eyes."
>
> Job 4:12–16

Notice that he said "a spirit," and not "the Spirit." Such demonic visitations are seldom explained in our churches, leaving believers unequipped and often shaken to the core. Only the church can provide adequate answers for the anxiety disorders that plague the planet. A congregation that is paralyzed by fear has lost its witness. "The wicked flee when no one is pursuing, but the righteous are bold as a lion" (Proverbs 28:1). That was not the case for the early church. "And when they had prayed, the place where they had gathered together was shaken, and they were filled with the Holy Spirit and began to speak the word of God with boldness" (Acts 4:31).

> I say this to bring to the clearest possible light the fact that it is our fear that lays us open to manipulation. Fear is the handle we ourselves give to those who would turn us around their will. Terrorism exists because we are afraid. There are international commissions that meet regularly to analyze the spread of terrorism and propose remedies. They are not likely to do away with the plague. The ultimate remedy lies in the human heart. Fearlessness alone can free us from the snares our own fears have built.[6]

SEVEN

Overcoming Depression

Dearest,

I feel certain I am going mad again. I feel we can't go through another of those terrible times. And I shan't recover this time. I begin to hear voices, and I can't concentrate. So I am doing what seems the best thing to do. You have given me the greatest possible happiness. You have been in every way all that anyone could be. I don't think two people could have been happier till this terrible disease came. I can't fight any longer.[1]

That was the suicide note that Virginia Woolf penned for her husband before she drowned herself in a river. It was also the opening scene in *The Hours*, a movie that intertwined three related stories of severely depressed people. The title is in reference to the hours and hours of never-ending agony that accompany depression. Her present circumstances were

This chapter is adapted from *Overcoming Depression*, which I coauthored with my wife, Joanne, who suffered with a life-threatening depression.

anything but negative, so why was she depressed? What are those "voices"?

Approximately eighteen million people in America (about 10 percent of all adults) will suffer from depression in any given year, according to the National Institutes of Health. Only a third of those people will seek treatment for their depression. David was said to have a whole heart for God, yet his numerous bouts of depression are recorded throughout the Psalms. Martin Luther battled depression most of his life. Abraham Lincoln said, "I am now the most miserable man living. If what I feel were equally distributed to the whole human family, there would not be one cheerful face on the earth."[2] Friends of Abraham Lincoln said of him, "He was a sad looking man; his melancholy dript from him as he walked,"[3] and "He was so overcome with mental depression that he never dare[d] carry a knife in his pocket."[4] Sir Winston Churchill referred to his own recurrent depression as the Black Dog. A biographer notes, "He had an enemy worthy of the word [Black Dog], an unambiguous tyrant whose destruction occupied him fully and invigorated him totally year in and year out."[5]

Let's face it, living in this fallen world can be depressing. Depression is a natural consequence when we experience losses in our lives. It is critically important that we understand how to respond to such losses, since everything we now possess someday we shall lose. It is God's intention that we grow through the trials of life and learn how to overcome feelings of helplessness and hopelessness. The richest treasures are often discovered in the deepest holes. What we need is the assurance that can only come from a God of all hope. Someone once said that we can live about forty days without food, about three days without water, and about eight minutes without air—but only one second without hope.

Physical Symptoms of Depression

Energy Level: *I just don't feel like doing anything.*

Lack of energy, excessive fatigue, and unrelenting tiredness are the characteristics of the melancholic. Walking, talking, cleaning the house, getting ready for work, or doing a project can take considerably longer time than usual. The lowered energy level and lowered interest in activities affect job performance. The severely depressed don't get dressed, and either stay in bed or lie around the house.

Sleep Disturbance: *I didn't sleep again last night!*

Having trouble sleeping is one of the most common symptoms of depression. Although some people feel like sleeping all of the time, it is more common to hear about insomnia. Initial insomnia (sleep onset insomnia) is the difficulty of falling asleep, which is more likely for those struggling with anxiety disorders. Depression is more commonly associated with terminal insomnia. They fall asleep out of sheer fatigue, but then wake up and can't get back to sleep. The inability to sleep contributes to the downward spiral of depression and leaves the sufferer with less energy for tomorrow.

Activity Level: *Why bother!*

Depression is accompanied by a decreased involvement in meaningful activities and having a lack of interest in life and commitment to follow through. Many find it difficult to pray because God seems like a distant figure.

Lack of Sex Drive: *Not tonight!*

Accompanying this loss of desire for sex is a wish for isolation, feelings of worthlessness, criticism of one's own appearance, loss of spontaneity, and apathy. The emotional state of depression usually creates problems in relationships, which obviously further curtails the desire to be intimate.

Somatic Complaint: *I ache all over!*

Many depressed people report physical aches and pains such as headaches, stomachache, and lower back pain, which can be quite severe. In a state of depression David wrote, "I am bowed down and brought very low; all day long I go about mourning. My back is filled with searing pain; there is no health in my body" (Psalm 38:6–7).

Loss of Appetite: *I'm not hungry!*

Depression is often accompanied by a decrease in appetite. However, in 20 percent of the cases, there is an increase of appetite and craving for food.

Mental and Emotional Symptoms

The most commonly known symptoms of depression are emotional. There are also resultant mental states that indicate severe to mild depression, but keep in mind that what a person thinks or believes is also a potential cause for depression. The following are the most common emotional symptoms and resultant mental states of those who are depressed:

Sadness: *I feel awful!*

Depression is most commonly characterized by a deep sadness. The "blues" seem to creep up slowly and bring with it a spirit of heaviness. Crying and brooding are common for those who are in a funk.

Despair: *It's hopeless!*

Despair is the absence of hope. Despair sees no light at the end of the tunnel, no hope at the end of the day, and no answers for the endless rounds of questions that plague the mind of the depressed. Three times the psalmists cried out, "Why are you in despair, O my soul? And why have you become disturbed within me? Hope in God, for I shall again praise Him, the help of my countenance and my God" (Psalm 42:5, 11; 43:5 NASB).

Irritability and Low Frustration Tolerance: *I have had it with you!* Depressed people have very little emotional reserve. Small things tick them off, and they are easily frustrated. They have a low tolerance level for the pressures of life.

Isolation and Withdrawal: *I'm going to my room!* People who suffer with depression pull away from others. They feel embarrassed to be with people when they feel so low. They don't want to be a wet blanket in the group and drag the others down by their depression. Although some may think that isolation is a viable short-term solution, avoidance often adds to the downward spiral of depression.

Negative Thought Patterns: *Nothing is working and I'm such a failure!* Depressed people generally have a negative view of themselves, their present circumstances, and the future. Such beliefs are more the cause than a symptom.

Thoughts of Suicide: *Everybody would be better off if I just died!* Sadness, isolation, loss of energy, strained relationships, and physical problems contaminate one's perspective of self and the future. Believing themselves to be helpless and hopeless, many begin to think of suicide as the only way out. It is the third leading cause of suicide for teenagers and ninth for adults.

Bipolar Depression

Depression is categorized as bipolar and unipolar. A bipolar, or manic-depressive, illness has two poles: highs (called manic moods) and lows (depressed moods). One of the foremost experts of this illness, Kay Jamison (she struggled with manic-depression herself), wrote *Touched With Fire*, a fascinating book revealing the fine line between genius and madness (mania). Some of the most creative people in the world struggled with this illness. These are just some of the names from the list that Jamison compiled:

Writers: Hans Christian Anderson, John Bunyan, Samuel Clemens, Ralph Waldo Emerson, William Faulkner,* Ernest Hemingway,* Herman Melville, Robert Louis Stevenson, Tennessee Williams,* Virginia Woolf.*

Composers: Irving Berlin,* Noel Coward, Stephen Foster, George Frideric Handel, Cole Porter,* Robert Schumann,* Peter Tchaikovsky.

Artists: Vincent van Gogh,* Michelangelo.

Those with an asterisk spent time in an asylum or psychiatric hospital. Ernest Hemingway, Virginia Woolf, and Vincent van Gogh committed suicide.[6] In her autobiography, *An Unquiet Mind*, Jamison describes her incredible accomplishments during her periods of mania. Treating her illness with lithium brought her relief but also decreased her creativity and productivity. She also said that taking medicine was not enough. She needed the objectivity of someone else to help her get through the depressive cycle.[7]

The transmission of a message through a brain cell requires a certain balance of sodium (positive) and chloride (negative) ions. Sodium chloride (NaCl) is a salt. In a similar fashion, electricity flows through copper better than it does through iron due to the chemical makeup of each substance. In a bipolar illness, the balance and polarity of positive and negative ions is abnormal. In depression the sodium ions increase by about 50 percent, and with the mania they increase as much as 200 percent. The drug of choice for bipolar depression has been lithium carbonate, which is an inert salt. This reduces the number of sodium and chloride ions, allowing the transmission to proceed through the cell and into other neurons. In such cases medicine is the primary answer, but I have seen God set free many people who were incorrectly labeled as bipolar.

Unipolar Depression

The focus on *medically* curing unipolar depression has been on the production, preservation, and transmission of neurotransmitters. Some of the earlier antidepressant drugs were monoamine oxidase inhibitors (MAOIs). The purpose of these medications is to block the action of monoamine oxidase, an enzyme that destroys certain neurotransmitters. Tricyclic antidepressants were the next generation of antidepressants. Their purpose is to keep the neurotransmitters in productive service longer. These were followed by selective serotonin reuptake inhibitors (SSRIs) such as Prozac and Lexapro. Unfortunately, stimulating the production of serotonin was not as selective as they thought. The brain will adapt to medications seeking balance, and an increase in serotonin may be accompanied by a decrease in dopamine. Such meds usually burst onto the scene with seemingly impressive results, but they slowly fade in popularity over the course of about ten years after a new crop of meds surfaces.

Antidepressant Medications

Serotonin is only one of forty different neurotransmitters, but it is the one most commonly linked to mood and the one most studied.

> Serotonin, or the lack of it, has been implicated not only in depression, uncontrollable appetite and obsessive-compulsive disorder but also in autism, bulimia, social phobias, premenstrual

syndrome, anxiety and panic, migraines, schizophrenia and even extreme violence."[8]

Serotonin-boosting medications currently make up the majority of doctors' prescriptions for depression. There is no way your doctor can accurately measure brain chemistry and the production of neurotransmitters. Prescribing antidepressants is somewhat of an educated guess:

> Despite years of study and impressive breakthroughs, researchers are only beginning to understand the chemical's complex role in the functioning of the body and brain—and how doctors can make adjustments when serotonin levels go out of balance. So far, the tools used to manipulate serotonin in the human brain are more like pharmacological machetes than they are like scalpels—crudely effective but capable of doing plenty of collateral damage. Says Barry Jacobs, a neuroscientist at Princeton University: "We just don't know enough about how the brain works."[9]

Even though medical doctors readily admit to a lack of precision, prescription drugs are their primary means of treating depression in the United States. Approximately fifty million Americans have been prescribed antidepressants. Julie Appleby reported for *USA Today* that the number of pharmaceutical representatives doubled from 41,800 in 1996 to 83,000 in 2000.[10] The strategy now is to go directly to the public with TV ads. "Ask a doctor for a prescription medication you saw advertised on TV, and 69 percent of the time you will go home with it."[11]

Each year, the FDA reviews about twenty-five new drugs for approval. For this task, the agency has a professional staff of fifteen hundred doctors, scientists, toxicologists, and statisticians. But to monitor the safety of the more than three thousand drugs already on the market and being prescribed to millions, the agency has a professional staff of just five doctors and one epidemiologist.[12] Because long-term monitoring is virtually non-existent, the then commissioner of the FDA, David Kessler, revealed that "only about 1% of serious events [side effects] are reported to the FDA."[13]

If you have been on an antidepressant for several months or years and believe you no longer need it, be sure to slowly sequence off the medication. Your brain has adapted to the medication. Those who go off too quickly may experience symptoms of withdrawal from the medication. That may reinforce the belief that you need the medication when in actuality you may not.

Electroconvulsive Therapy (ECT)

Electroconvulsive therapy, or shock treatment as it is commonly called, is used to treat severe cases of endogenous depression in patients that are not responsive to medication. It is one of the most misunderstood and questioned medical treatments for mental illness due primarily to perceived abuses in the past. ECT administers a small electrical shock to the brain that induces a convulsion. Muscle relaxants and a mild anesthetic are given to the patient so that the seizures are only slightly felt by the patient. They usually experience a mild amnesia with very little pain. The one occasional side effect is a short-term memory loss. Nobody knows why, but it seems to stimulate the production of neurotransmitters. In some cases it is more effective than antidepressants and it works faster with fewer side effects, but it isn't considered a long-term answer. Most physicians would still see ECT as a last resort.

Toward a Complete Solution

If you read only this far, you could easily conclude that depression can be cured simply by taking the right medications. That would be unfortunate and very inaccurate. Medications cannot change your circumstances or cause you to resolve personal and spiritual conflicts, but they may have the potential to jump-start the computer so the proper program can run.

Psychologist Dr. David Antonuccio and his colleagues at the University of Nevada School of Medicine in Reno found in their research that, "despite the conventional wisdom, the data suggests that there is no stronger medicine than psychotherapy in the treatment of depression, even if severe."[14] *Consumer Reports* recently reached similar conclusions. After four thousand of its subscribers responded to the largest-ever survey on the use of therapy and/or drugs to treat depression, researchers at the Consumers Union determined that "psychotherapy alone worked as well as psychotherapy combined with medication, like Prozac and Xanax. Most people who took the drugs did feel they were helpful, but many reported side effects."[15] Imagine what that research would have revealed if all the therapy was Christ-centered!

Such research brings up the critical question of causation. Which came first, external negative circumstances, poor mental evaluation of life, lack of faith in God, or the chemical imbalance? A depressed mood will likely accompany biochemistry changes in the body, but to say that changed biochemistry caused depression is as incomplete as saying a dead battery caused the car not to start. We would have to ask, what caused the battery to fail, and is there another reason that the car wouldn't start? Is the car out of gas? Was it a faulty alternator or a broken belt? Were the lights left on? Is the battery old and worn out? You can jump-start the car by using booster cables, which would be enough if you had just left the lights on. A good mechanic would consider many other causes to ensure that the car would continue to run.

The fact that antidepressant medications help depressed people feel better is not even arguable. They do. On the other hand, taking medications every time you have a symptom of depression is like getting a jump-start every time your car won't start. The car is designed to function as a whole unit, and so are we. After having been on an antidepressant medication for almost three weeks, one woman declared, "I didn't know the promises in the Bible were true for me until now." The proper use of medication enabled her to assume a responsible course of action. Martin Seligman, a noted researcher on depression, reflected on its causes:

> I have spent the last twenty years trying to learn what causes depression. Here is what I think. Bipolar depression (manic-depression) is an illness of the body, biological in origin and containable by drugs. Some unipolar depressions, too, are partly biological, particularly the fiercest ones. Some unipolar depression is inherited. If one of two identical twins is depressed, the other is somewhat more likely to be depressed than if they'd been fraternal twins. This kind of unipolar depression can often be contained with drugs, although not nearly as successfully as bipolar depression can be, and its symptoms can often be relieved by electroconvulsive therapy.
>
> But inherited unipolar depressions are in the minority. This raises the question of where the great number of depressions making up the epidemic in this country come from. I ask myself if human beings have undergone physical changes over the century that have made them more vulnerable to depression. Probably not. It is very doubtful that our brain chemistry or our genes have changed radically over the last two generations. So a tenfold increase in depression is not likely to be explained on biological grounds.
>
> I suspect that the epidemic depression so familiar to all of us is best viewed as psychological. My guess is that most depression starts with problems in living and with specific ways of thinking about these problems.[16]

I generally agree with Seligman, but I disagree that all severe unipolar and bipolar depression is only a physical illness of the body. It certainly can be the problem, and physical and chemical imbalances should definitely be considered in severe cases. But we have found that many severe depressions have a spiritual component, which is overlooked in the secular world and often in our churches. To illustrate this point, read the following testimony:

> I am writing in regard to your seminar in Minnesota. The day it was to start, I was to be admitted to a hospital for the fifth time for manic-depression. I have been dealing with this for almost two years. We had gone to several doctors and tried about every drug they could think of. I also had shock treatments. I attempted suicide twice. Unable to work any longer, I spent most of my days downstairs wishing I were dead or planning my next attempt. Also, it was a good place to protect myself from people and the world around me. I had a history of self-abuse. I have spent thirty-odd years in jail or prisons. I was a drug addict and an alcoholic. I have been in drug and alcohol treatment twenty-eight times.
>
> I became a Christian several years ago but always lived a defeated life. Now I was going back to the hospital to try new medications or more shock treatments. My wife and friends convinced me your seminar would be of more value. The hospital was concerned because they believed I needed medical help. As the four days of the conference progressed, my head started to clear up! The Word of God was ministering to me, even though I was confused and in pain. I told one of your staff that I was in my eleventh hour. He set up an appointment for me.
>
> The session lasted seven hours. They didn't leave one stone uncovered. The session was going great until I came to bitterness and unforgiveness. The three things that motivated my life were low self-esteem, anger, and bitterness, which were the result of being molested by a priest and suffering from many years of physical and verbal abuse in my childhood. I can honestly say I forgave them, and God moved right in, lifting my depression. My eyes were now open to God's truth. I felt lighter than ever before.

I did go to the hospital, but after two days they said I didn't need to be there. My doctors said I was a different person. They had never seen a person change so fast. They said, "Whatever you are doing, don't stop." I have been growing in the Lord daily. There is so much before Christ and after Christ that I could go on for forever.

Secular counselors seldom, if ever, see that kind of resolution. Too many people continue in their depression because they have considered only one possible cause and therefore only one possible cure. It would be a tragedy for a godly pastor or Christ-centered counselor to try helping a person who is physically sick without suggesting some medical attention. On the other hand, for medical doctors to think that they can cure the whole person with medication is equally tragic.

Steps to Overcoming Depression

Recovery begins by saying, "I have a problem and I need help." There are adequate answers for depression, but you have to want to get well and be willing to do whatever it takes to do it. The key to any cure is commitment. I offer the following sequential order for overcoming depression.

First: Submit to God and resist the devil (Matthew 6:33; James 4:7)

God can do wonders with a broken heart if you give Him all the pieces. In our Western world we have been conditioned to seek every possible natural explanation and cure first. When that is not successful, *then there is nothing more that we can do but pray*. Scripture has a different order. "But seek first his kingdom and his righteousness, and all these things will be given to you as well" (Matthew 6:33). The first thing a Christian should do about anything is pray, which is what we do in the Steps to Freedom in Christ. The process is intended to help you resolve any conflicts that may exist between you and your heavenly Father through repentance and faith in Him. Essentially, the process helps you submit to God and resist the devil (see James 4:7). Doing so eliminates the influence of the evil one and connects you with God in a personal and powerful way. Now by the grace of God you will be able to process the remaining steps for overcoming depression.

Second: Commit your body to God as a living sacrifice (Romans 12:1)

After you have consulted the Great Physician, a visit to your doctor may be in order. Depression is a multifaceted problem that affects the body, soul, and spirit. Consequently, a comprehensive cure for depression will require a wholistic answer. There are many forms of biological depression that can be diagnosed and treated. A disorder of the endocrine system can produce depressive symptoms. The endocrine system includes the thyroid, parathyroid, thymus, pancreas, and adrenal glands. The endocrine system produces hormones that are released directly into the bloodstream. The thyroid gland controls metabolism. An under-active thyroid (hypothyroidism) will cause changes in mood, including depression. The metabolism of sugar is especially important for maintaining physical and emotional stability. Hypoglycemia (low blood sugar) will likely be accompanied with emotional instability.

The fact that women suffer from depression more than men may be due to their biological nature (or it may have something to do with who they are living with!). Archibald Hart said,

> The reproductive organs of the female are extremely prone to creating mood swings. The depression at the onset of menstruation, the premenstrual syndrome (PMS), the use of contraceptive pills,

pregnancy, postpartum reactions, and menopause all revolve around the female's reproductive system. And as we currently understand it, the system is fraught with depression pitfalls.[17]

Many of the symptoms of biological depression can also be eliminated when we assume our responsibility to live a balanced life of rest, exercise, and diet. To live a healthy life, we must be health oriented, not illness oriented. It is the same dynamic of winning the battle for your mind. The answer is not to renounce all the lies. The answer is to choose the truth. But if you aren't aware that there are lies, and if you ignore what your body is telling you, then you will likely fall victim to disease and the father of lies. Whenever you start to sense that you are physically and mentally slipping back into a depression, don't just succumb to it, take charge of your life by praying as follows:

Dear heavenly Father, I submit myself to you as your child, and I declare myself to be totally dependent upon you. I yield my body to you as a living sacrifice, and I ask you to fill me with your Holy Spirit. I renounce the lies of the evil one, and I choose to believe the truth as revealed in your Word. I resist the devil and command all evil spirits to leave my presence. I now commit myself to you and my body to you as an instrument of righteousness. In Jesus' precious name I pray. Amen.

Third: Be transformed by the renewing of your mind

Depression can be divided into two categories. One is related to lifestyle and the other is precipitated by some crisis event. Lifestyle depression can be traced to early childhood development or living in an oppressive situation that created or communicated a sense of hopelessness and helplessness. Over time our minds have been programmed to think negatively about ourselves, our circumstances, and the future. These negative thoughts and lies are often deeply ingrained. There have been thousands of mental rehearsals that have added to the feelings you are experiencing right now. The natural tendency is to ruminate on these negative thoughts. Daniel Goleman said, "One of the main determinants of whether a depressed mood will persist or lift is the degree to which people ruminate. Worrying about what's depressing us, it seems, makes the depression all the more intense and prolonged."[18]

Changing false beliefs and attitudes is necessary to overcome depression. The world will put you down, and the devil will accuse you, but you don't have to believe either one. You have to take every thought captive to the obedience of Christ. In other words, you have to believe the truth as revealed in God's Word. You don't overcome the father of lies by research or by reason; you overcome deceiving spirits by revelation. God is not going to remove us from the negativity of this fallen world. We are sanctified and protected by the truth of God's Word. Jesus said, "I have told you these things, so that in me you may have peace. In this world you will have trouble. But take heart! I have overcome the world" (John 16:33). Renewing our minds with truth will not continue if you don't actively work to sustain it. Every mental stronghold that is torn down in Christ makes the next one easier. Every thought you take captive makes the next one more likely to surrender. Lifestyle depression is the result of repeated blows that come from living in a fallen world. Rehearsing the truth again and again is the key to renewing your mind.

Fourth: Commit yourself to good behavior

We are not instantly delivered from lifestyle depression. We have to grow out of it. It takes time to renew our minds, but it doesn't take time to change our behavior, which facilitates the process of renewing our minds as well as positively affecting how we feel. We don't feel our way into good behavior; we behave our way into good feelings. If you wait until you feel like doing what is right, you will likely never do it. Jesus said, "Now that you know these things, you will be blessed if you do them" (John 13:17).

That is why some interventions for depression focus on behavior. Depressed people are helped to schedule appointments and activities that pull them out of their negative mood. Go to work even though you may not feel like getting out of bed. Plan an activity and stick to it. Get more physical exercise and commit yourself to follow through on your plans. You may *feel* tired, but your body needs exercise. Start with a low-impact aerobic program or take walks with friends and family members. Continue routine duties even though you feel like you don't have the energy. These behavioral interventions or activities are only a start in developing a healthy lifestyle. If these are too difficult or physically impossible, then seek the kind of physical therapy that will get you back on your feet.

Stop living to eat and start eating properly to live. Balance your diet with 60 percent good carbohydrates, 30 percent proteins, and 10 percent healthy fats. Try to avoid processed sugars and high-fructose corn syrup. Take a multivitamin and be sure that it includes vitamin D and B-complex vitamins, especially B-12. B-complex vitamins help the adrenal glands deal with stress, and they are water soluble, so they aren't stored in your system.

There are certain negative behaviors that will only contribute to depression. Drowning out your sorrows with drugs and alcohol is at the top of this destructive list. Although this may bring temporary relief, it will only further contribute to the depression.

Fifth: Seek meaningful relationships

One of the major symptoms of depression is withdrawal from meaningful relationships. Isolating ourselves and being alone with our negative thoughts will only contribute to the downward spiral. You may feel like you want to be alone, but you need to stay connected to God and in contact with the right people. We absolutely need God, and we necessarily need each other. Wrong associations and relationships, however, will only pull you down. "Do not be misled: 'Bad company corrupts good character'" (1 Corinthians 15:33).

A frog was frolicking with his friends when another frog rubbed him the wrong way. Straying off from the pack, he hopped into a rut in the road. Two days later he was still stuck in the rut. Some old friends came bouncing by and encouraged him to hop out of the rut, but he remained stuck in the rut. Two days later the friends saw him hopping around the pasture, and they asked what brought about the change. The frog said, "A Mack Truck came along and I had to get out of there!" Sometimes we need someone or something to shake us out of our lethargy.

Sixth: Overcome your losses

A loss can be real, or it can be threatened or imagined— often a negative thought or lie that is believed. Either one can precipitate a depression. How we respond to any loss or crisis will determine how fast we recover. The following steps will help you overcome your losses:

1. Identify each loss

Concrete losses are easier to recognize than abstract losses. Changing jobs and moving to a new location can precipitate a depression even though it could improve your social status and financial base. The move may mean the loss of friends, community, and church. It will take some time to build new friendships and become part of a new church family. Many losses are multifaceted. For instance, the concrete loss of a job and wages may be accompanied by the abstract losses of self-respect, sense of worth, and collegial relationships. People react differently to losses because people have different values and different levels of maturity. In order to get beyond denial and into the grieving process, you must understand what it is that you are losing or have already lost.

2. Separate concrete losses from abstract losses

Concrete losses are tangible, while abstract losses relate more to personal goals, dreams, and ideas. Abstract losses relate deeply to who we are and why we are here. Many concrete losses, such as the loss of a job, are contaminated with abstract losses. You may find a new job next week but remain depressed because you feel the pain of rejection and wrongly believe you are a failure. That is another reason why it is so important to understand who we are in Christ and find our acceptance, security, and significance in Him.

3. Separate real from imagined or threatened losses

You cannot process an imagined or threatened loss in the same way you can a real one. In a real loss you can face the truth, grieve the loss, and make the necessary changes that make it possible to go on living in a meaningful way. A lawyer heard a rumor that his firm was going to be sued for services he performed. He thought, "I'm ruined. The firm is going down and it is all my fault." Such thinking led to a major depression and antidepressant medications. I saw him a year later, and the company hadn't been sued. It had just been imagined.

4. Convert imagined and threatened losses to real losses

Imagined losses are distortions of reality. They are based on suspicions or lies that we have believed or presumptions that we have made. The mind doesn't like vacuums and will make assumptions when we don't know the facts. Seldom does the mind assume the best. We don't always act upon our assumptions, but if we do, we shall be counted among the fools, because through presumption comes nothing but strife (see Proverbs 13:10). People ruminate various possibilities and consequences in their minds until they are depressed. The answer is to verify these assumptions and then follow Peter's advice: "Cast all your anxiety on him because he cares for you. Be self-controlled and alert. Your enemy the devil prowls around like a roaring lion looking for someone to devour. Resist him, standing firm in your faith" (1 Peter 5:7–8).

Threatened losses have the potential for being real losses. They include such things as the possibility of a layoff at work, or a spouse who threatens to leave you. Such threats can precipitate a depression. I find it helpful to think what the worst-case scenario may be and then ask myself the question, "Can I live with it?" The answer is always yes. Essentially, you are processing the threat in your mind as a real loss. The threat no longer has any power over you, and in that way you are not letting any person or event determine who you are or keep you from being the person God created you to be.

5. Facilitate the grieving process

The natural response to any crisis is to first deny that it is really happening, then get angry that it did happen, then try to alter the situation by bargaining with God or others. When that doesn't work, you feel depressed. You cannot bypass the grieving process, but you can shorten it by allowing yourself to feel the full force of the loss. The fact that certain losses are depressing is reality. It hurts to lose something that has value to you. You cannot fully process your loss until you feel its full force. That is probably what Jesus had in mind when He said, "Blessed are those who mourn, for they will be comforted" (Matthew 5:4).

6. Face the reality of the loss

Only after you have faced its full impact are you ready to deal with the reality of the loss. This is the critical juncture. Are you going to resign from life, succumb to the depression, and drop out, or are you going to accept what you cannot change and let go of the loss? You can feel sorry for yourself for the rest of your life, or you can decide to live with your loss and learn how to go on in a meaningful way. A prolonged depression signifies an overattachment to people, places, and things that we had no right or ability to control.

7. Develop a biblical perspective on the loss

The trials and tribulations of life are intended to produce proven character. We suffer for the sake of righteousness. We can potentially come through any crisis a better person than the one we were before. Losses are inevitable and are not intended to destroy us, but they will reveal who we are. People have discovered or deepened the awareness of who they are in Christ as a direct result of losses. Each subsequent loss only deepens that reality, perfects our character, and prepares us for an even greater ministry. We are all going to be victimized by losses and abuses. We could drown in our own pity, blame others, claim that life isn't fair, and stay depressed the rest of our lives. Whether we remain a victim is our choice. "For we who live are constantly being delivered over to death for Jesus' sake, so that the life of Jesus also may be manifested in our mortal flesh" (2 Corinthians 4:11 NASB).

8. Let go of the past

A woman shared that her best friend ran off with her husband ten years earlier. She was deeply hurt by this incredible betrayal. She thought her life was ruined by those adulterers, and there was nothing she could do about it. For ten years she smoldered in bitterness and depression. Feelings of resentment and plots of revenge ruminated in her mind. I told her, "I see you with one fist extended up to heaven, where God has a firm grip on you. Your other fist is hanging on to your past, and you aren't about to let go. You are not even hanging on to God, but your heavenly Father is hanging on to you, His beloved child. Isn't it time to let it go? You are only hurting yourself." At the end of the conference she worked through the Steps, and she let it go. The next morning she was singing in the choir with the countenance of a liberated child of God.

Once I held in my tightly clenched fist . . . ashes. Ashes from a burn inflicted upon my ten-year-old body. Ashes I didn't ask for. The scar was forced on me.

And for seventeen years the fire smoldered. I kept my fist closed in secret, hating those ashes, yet unwilling to release them. Not sure if I could. Not convinced it was worth it. Marring the things I touched and leaving black marks everywhere . . . or so it seemed.

I tried to undo it all, but the marks were always there to remind me that I couldn't. I really couldn't. But God could! His sweet Holy Spirit spoke to my heart one night in tearful desperation. He whispered, "I want to give you beauty for your ashes, the oil of joy for your mourning and the garment of praise for your spirit of heaviness."

I had never heard of such a trade as this: Beauty? Beauty for ashes? My sadly stained memory for the healing in His word? My soot-like dreams for His songs in the night? My helpless and hurting emotions for His ever-constant peace?

How could I be so stubborn as to refuse an offer such as this? So willingly, yet in slow motion, and yes, while sobbing, I opened my bent fingers and let the ashes drop to the ground. In silence, I heard the wind blow them away. Away from me . . . forever. I am now able to place my open hands gently around the fist of another hurting soul and say with confidence, "Let them go. There really is beauty beyond your comprehension. Go ahead—trust Him. His beauty for your ashes."

Author Unknown

EIGHT

Overcoming
Sexual Strongholds

On November 21, 2003, I was watching the Sunday evening program *60 Minutes*. One segment was on adult entertainment, which I didn't particularly care to watch, but I thought I better. I ended up downloading a hard copy of the report, because I was so astonished by what they said. In summary:

- $10,000,000,000 was spent every year on adult entertainment, and "reputable" industries were cashing in because the profit margin was so high.
- There were 800 million rentals of adult video tapes and DVDs in video stores.
- In 2002 the porn industry produced 11,000 titles.
- The porn industry employed (at the time) 12,000 people in California alone.

- 50 percent of the guests at major hotels used pay-per-view porn, which accounted for 75 percent of their video profits.
- Type in the word *sex* in a search engine like Google and you would get 180 million hits. Since 2003 the number has more than quadrupled.

The Centers for Disease Control reported in 2000 that "in the United States, more than 65 million people are currently living with a sexually transmitted disease (STD). An additional 15 million people would become infected with one or more STDs each year, roughly half of whom contract life-long infections."[1] The pandemic has not decreased. In 2008 there were 110 million Americans who had an STD, and the number was increasing by 20 million a year.

David Foster, the child of a Presbyterian pastor, gained some fame as an actor who wasn't acting when he doubled as a male prostitute. Life in the gutter finally drove him to Christ, and he has become a powerful witness for sexual freedom and healing through his ministry, Mastering Life Ministries. According to David's research, if there are sixteen people sitting in one row in any church, two will be struggling with their sexual orientation. They are not gay, but the enemy is presenting an intense battle for their minds. Four of the sixteen people have been sexually abused. The "official" estimate is one out of every four women and one out of every seven men, but that is based only on what is reported. The more likely scenario is that one out of every three women and one out of every four men have been sexually abused. In the same pew of sixteen people, an additional four have unresolved sexual strongholds, and that is true of every row in every church in America.

I surveyed the student body of a good conservative seminary and discovered that 60 percent of the male student body was struggling with sexual guilt. Of that group, 50 percent said they would take an elective that would help them overcome sexual strongholds if confidentiality was ensured. It wasn't offered! Imagine sending into the world seminary graduates who can't free themselves from their own sexual struggles, much less help others. We can't be an effective disciple-making church without helping God's children overcome sexual strongholds, and we don't accomplish that by watering down God's standards.

The Entrapment of Sin

Can we live a righteous life? Can we make a choice not to sin? In Romans 6:1–13 Paul argues that we can because of our identity and position in Christ. It is important to note that the verb tenses in Romans 6:1–10 are all past tense. There are no imperatives to obey. There are only indicatives to believe.

Paul begins by asking, "What shall we say then? Are we to continue in sin so that grace may increase? May it never be! How shall we who died to sin still live in it?" (vv. 1–2 NASB). You may be tempted to ask, "How do I die to sin?" You can't, because you died to sin the moment you were born again.

"We were therefore buried with him through baptism into death in order that, just as Christ was raised from the dead through the glory of the Father, we too may live a new life. If we have been united with him like this in his death, we will certainly also be united with him in his resurrection" (vv. 4–5). You cannot identify with the death and burial of Christ without also identifying with His resurrection and ascension. You have died with Christ, *and* you have been raised with Him, and you are seated with Him in the heavenlies (see Ephesians 2:6). From this position you have all the authority and power you need to live the Christian life. Every child of God is spiritually alive "in Christ" and is identified with Him:

- in His death (Romans 6:3, 6; Galatians 2:20; Colossians 3:1–3)
- in His burial (Romans 6:4)
- in His resurrection (Romans 6:5, 8, 11)
- in His ascension (Ephesians 2:6)
- in His life (Romans 5:10–11)
- in His power (Ephesians 1:19–20)
- in His inheritance (Romans 8:16–17; Ephesians 1:11–12)

Paul continues in Romans, "Knowing this, that our old self was crucified with Him, in order that our body of sin might be done away with, so that we would no longer be slaves to sin" (6:6 NASB). Your *old self* was (past tense) crucified with Christ. The only proper response to this powerful truth is to believe it. You may be tempted to ask, "What experience must I have in order for this to be true?" We don't make anything true by our experience. We choose to believe what God has already accomplished for us and to live accordingly by faith— then it works out in our experience. It is not what we do that determines who we are—it is who we are and what we believe that determines what we do. We don't labor in God's vineyard hoping that He may someday love us. God already loves us, so we joyfully labor in His vineyard.

"Anyone who has died has been freed from sin" (v. 7). Have you died with Christ? Then you are free from sin. "But I don't feel free from sin." If you only believe what you feel, you will never live a victorious life. You are not being hypocritical if you live contrary to how you feel. That is what the devil wants you to believe. You are being hypocritical if you are living contrary to what you profess to believe.

"If we died with Christ, we believe that we will also live with him. For we know that since Christ was raised from the dead, he cannot die again; death no longer has mastery over him" (vv. 8–9). Death has no mastery over us, but what about sin? Paul continues, "The death he died, he died to sin once for all; but the life he lives, he lives to God" (v. 10). This was accomplished when "God made him who had no sin to be sin for us, so that in him we might become the righteousness of God" (2 Corinthians 5:21). Since you are alive in Him, you are also dead to sin.

Many Christians accept the truth that Christ died for the sins they have already committed, but what about the sins they commit in the future? When Christ died for all your sins, how many of your sins were then future? All of them! This is not a license to sin, or to make grace increase, but is a marvelous truth on which to live a righteous life and stand against Satan's accusations.

In Romans 6:11, Paul summarizes how we are to respond to what Christ has accomplished for us by His death and resurrection: "In the same way, count yourselves dead to sin but alive to God in Christ Jesus." We do not make ourselves dead to sin by considering it to be so. We consider ourselves dead to sin because God says it already is so. The verb *count* is present tense. In other words, we must continuously believe this truth and daily affirm that we are dead to sin and alive in Christ. We don't have to sin, but we will, since we are considerably less than perfect. We are saints who sin, but we do so less and less as we mature in Christ. John wrote, "My little children, I am writing these things to you so that you may not sin. And if anyone sins, we have an advocate with the Father, Jesus Christ the righteous" (1 John 2:1 NASB). We also have an adversary ready to accuse us.

Death is the ending of a relationship, but not existence. Sin is still powerful and appealing, and death is still imminent, but our relationship with both has changed because of our union with Christ. Paul explains how this is possible in Romans 8:1–2: "There is now no condemnation for those who are in Christ Jesus, because through Christ Jesus the law of the Spirit of life set me free from the law of sin and death."

A law cannot be done away with, but it can be overcome by a greater law—"the law of the Spirit of life in Christ Jesus." To illustrate, we cannot humanly fly in our own power, because the law of gravity keeps us bound to earth. But we *can* fly in an airplane, which has the power to overcome the law of gravity. We cannot humanly stop sinning in our own strength, because the power of sin keeps us in bondage. But if we live by faith according to what God says is true in the power of the Holy Spirit, we will not carry out the desires of the flesh. The importance of knowing who we are "in Christ" cannot be overstated

We believe what God has accomplished for us, and that He will remain faithful, but we have a part to play as well. Paul continues, "Therefore do not let sin reign in your mortal body so that you obey its lusts" (Romans 6:12 NASB). According to this verse, it is our responsibility to not allow sin to reign in our mortal bodies. How can we do that? Paul answers in verse 13 (NASB): "Do not go on presenting the members of your body to sin as instruments of unrighteousness; but present yourselves to God as those alive from the dead, and your members as instruments of righteousness to God." Notice that there is only one negative action to avoid, and two positive actions to practice.

Don't present the members of your body to sin. We are not to use our eyes, hands, feet, or any part of our bodies in any way that would serve sin. When you see a sexually explicit program on TV and lustfully watch it, you are offering your body to sin. When you get inappropriately touchy-feely with a co-worker of the opposite sex, you are offering your body to sin. When you fantasize sexually about someone other than your spouse, you are offering your body to sin. Whenever you choose to offer parts of your body to sin, you invite sin to rule in your physical body.

Offer yourselves and members of your body to God. Notice that Paul makes a distinction between "yourselves" and "members of your body." Self is who we are on the inside—the immaterial or inner person that is being renewed day by day (see 2 Corinthians 4:16). So dedicate yourself to God, and commit your body to God as an instrument of righteousness. If you use your body as an instrument of unrighteousness, you will allow sin to reign in your mortal body. There is no way that you could commit a sexual sin without using your body as an instrument of unrighteousness; therefore, committing a sexual sin allows sin to reign in your mortal body. That is why Paul wrote, "I urge you, brethren, by the mercies of God, to present your bodies a living and holy sacrifice, acceptable to God, which is your spiritual service of worship" (Romans 12:1 NASB). If you do that first, then you will be more successful doing the next verse that instructs us to be transformed by the renewing of our minds. In 1 Corinthians 6:13–20, Paul offers a little more body theology, especially as it relates to sexual immorality:

> The body is not meant for sexual immorality, but for the Lord, and the Lord for the body. By his power God raised the Lord from the dead, and he will raise us also. Do you not know that your bodies are members of Christ himself? Shall I then take the members of Christ and unite them with a prostitute? Never! Do you not know that he who unites himself with a prostitute is one with her in body? For it is said, "The two will become one flesh." But he who unites himself with the Lord is one with him in spirit. Flee from sexual immorality. All other sins a man commits are outside his body, but he who sins sexually sins against his own body. Do you not know that your body is a temple of the Holy Spirit, who is in you, whom you have

received from God? You are not your own; you were bought at a price. Therefore honor God with your body.

This passage teaches that we have more than a spiritual union with God. Our bodies are members of Christ himself. Romans 8:11 declares, "If the Spirit of him who raised Jesus from the dead is living in you, he who raised Christ from the dead will also give life to your mortal bodies through his Spirit, who lives in you." Our bodies are actually God's temple because His Spirit dwells in us. To use our bodies for sexual immorality is to defile the temple of God.

It is hard for us to fully understand the moral outrage felt in heaven when one of God's children uses His temple as an instrument of unrighteousness. It is even worse when someone defiles the temple of another person through rape or incest. It compares with the despicable act of Antiochus Epiphanes in the second century before Christ. This godless Syrian ruler overran Jerusalem, declared the Mosaic ceremonies illegal, erected a statue of Zeus in the temple, and slaughtered a pig—an unclean animal—on the altar. Can you imagine how God's people must have felt to have their holy place so thoroughly desecrated? Have you ever felt the same way about defiling God's temple that is our bodies?

What happens when a child of God—who is united with the Lord and one spirit with Him—also unites with another through sexual immorality? The Bible says they become one flesh. They bond together. I can't fully explain it, but I have certainly seen the negative effect of such unions. Bonding is a positive thing in a wholesome relationship, but in an immoral union, bonding only leads to bondage.

How many times have you heard of a Christian young woman become involved with an immoral man, have sex with him, and then continue in a sick relationship? He mistreats her, and friends and relatives tell her, "He's no good for you. Get rid of the bum!" But she won't listen to them. Why? Because a spiritual and emotional bond has been formed. The two of them have become one flesh. Such bonds can only be broken in Christ.

In the Steps to Freedom in Christ, we invite inquirers to pray, asking the Lord to reveal to their minds every sexual use of their bodies as instruments of unrighteousness. God does, and He usually starts with their first experience, which may be incest or rape. Then for each one God brings to mind, they pray, "I renounce that use of my body [having sex] with [the person's name], and I ask you to break that sexual bond spiritually, mentally, and emotionally." Then they give their bodies to God as living sacrifices and pray that God would fill them with His Holy Spirit. Finally, they are encouraged to forgive those who have offended them. They forgive others for their own sakes, since nothing will keep them more bound to their past than unforgiveness.

In the cases of rape and incest, a person's temple is also defiled, even though he or she is the victim. "Not fair!" you say. Of course it isn't fair—it is a violation of that person's temple, like Antiochus Epiphanes' violation of the temple at Jerusalem, and the Maccabees who tried to stop him were martyred. People who have been victimized don't have to remain victims. They can renounce that use of their body and give it to God as a living sacrifice.

I was asked by a local pastor to counsel a young woman who was hearing voices. They were so real to her that she couldn't understand why we couldn't hear them. She had lived with a man who had abused her and peddled drugs for a living. She was now living at home but was still attached to him. Near the beginning of the session I asked her what she would do if we asked her to make a commitment to never see him again. She said, "I would probably get up and leave." I suspected that would be the case, but I wanted the pastor to hear it, and I want you to hear it. Having her make such a commitment was a legitimate goal, but the timing was wrong.

After hearing her story, I asked if she would like to resolve the problems she was having in her life. She agreed, and I led her through the Steps. She renounced having sex with this man and others; asked God to break the sexual, mental, emotional, and spiritual bonds; and committed her body to God as a living sacrifice. When we were done, there were no more demonic voices, and she seemed to be in complete peace. She had confessed her sin numerous times before without any sense of relief. Confession is the first step in repentance, but doing that alone will not bring resolution. I was sharing with her how to maintain her freedom when she remarked, "I am never going to see that man again." That conviction came from God, but it hadn't come until she had fully repented. She also had no success in winning the battle for her mind before, but now she could, which is a critical part of maintaining her freedom, because the flesh patterns are still there.

Winning the Battle for Our Minds

Those who have deeply ingrained flesh patterns leading to addictive behaviors struggle the most with temptation, and the devil knows which buttons to push.

> So, if you think you are standing firm, be careful that you don't fall! No temptation has seized you except what is common to man. And God is faithful; he will not let you be tempted beyond what you can bear. But when you are tempted, he will also provide a way out so that you can stand up under it.
>
> 1 Corinthians 10:12–13

Jesus showed us the "way out" when He was tempted by Satan. After He had fasted for forty days and nights, the Holy

Spirit led Him into the wilderness (see Matthew 4:1–4). That is as vulnerable as anyone can be. He was on the verge of starvation and alone in the wilderness. The temptation for Jesus to turn the rock into bread was a real temptation for the flesh. Temptations appeal to legitimate needs that we all have but steer us away from the One who will meet all our needs according to His riches. The devil wanted Jesus to use His divine attributes independent of the Father in order to save His physical life. That was the same temptation that came through the mouth of Peter that prompted Jesus to say, "Get behind Me, Satan! You are a stumbling block to me; for you are not setting your mind on God's interests, but man's" (Matthew 16:23 NASB).

Jesus quoted Scripture in all three temptations, but what is often overlooked is that He said it aloud. Satan is under no obligation to obey our thoughts, because He doesn't perfectly know them. Our protective armor includes "the sword of the Spirit, which is the word [*rhema*] of God" (Ephesians 6:17 NASB). There is an important reason that Paul used *rhema* instead of *logos*. *Logos* refers more to the content or character of the Word, whereas *rhema* refers to the speaking of God's Word. Those who struggle with addictive behavior are most vulnerable when they are alone in front of their computer, in a hotel room, etc. In such cases they won't feel embarrassed to verbally resist the devil. Say it! "Lord, fill me with your Holy Spirit, and in the name of Jesus I command Satan to leave me." Doing so has kept me free on my many road trips. For the times when you are with others, mentally choose the truth.

When I was a young Christian, I decided to clean up my mind. I had a relatively good upbringing, for which I am thankful, but I didn't become a Christian until my midtwenties. After four years in the navy, my mind was polluted with a lot of junk. I had seen enough pornography aboard ship to plague me for years. Images would dance in my mind for months after one look. I hated it. I struggled every time I went to a place where pornography was available.

When I made the decision to clean up my mind, do you think the battle got easier or harder? It got harder, of course. Temptation isn't much of a battle if you easily give in to it. It is fierce when you decide to stand against it. Think of your polluted mind as a pot filled with stale black coffee. It is dark and smelly. There is no way to get the pollution of coffee out of the liquid, because there is no Delete button. However, sitting beside the coffeepot is a huge bowl of crystal-clear ice, which represents the Word of God. Your goal is to purify the contents of the pot by adding ice cubes to it every day. I wish there was a way to dump all the cubes (words of the Bible) in at one time, but there isn't. Every cube dilutes the mixture, making it a little purer. You can only put in one or two cubes a day, so the process seems almost futile at first. But over the course of time, the water begins to look less and less polluted, and the taste and smell of coffee decreases. The process continues to work provided you don't add more coffee grounds. If you read your Bible and then look at pornography, you are treading water at best.

Paul writes, "Let the peace of Christ rule in your hearts, since as members of one body you were called to peace. And be thankful" (Colossians 3:15). How do we rid ourselves of evil thoughts, purify our minds, and allow the peace of Christ to reign? The answer is found in the next verse: "Let the word of Christ dwell in you richly" (v. 16).

The psalmist gives similar instruction: "How can a young man keep his way pure? By living according to your word. I seek you with all my heart; do not let me stray from your commands. I have hidden your word in my heart that I might not sin against you" (Psalm 119:9–11). Merely trying to stop thinking bad thoughts won't work. We must fill our minds with the clear

Word of God. There is no alternative plan. We overcome the father of lies by choosing the truth!

You may find that winning the battle for your mind will initially be two steps forward and one step back. Gradually it will become three steps forward and one step back, then four and five steps forward as you learn to take every thought captive and make it obedient to Christ. You may despair with all your steps backward, but God won't give up on you. Remember, your sins are already forgiven. This is a winnable battle, because you are alive in Christ and dead to sin. The bigger war has already been won by Christ. We have mop-up duty with orders to occupy until He returns.

Homosexual Strongholds

While I was speaking at a camp, a mother called and asked if she and her twelve-year-old son could spend an hour with me. The husband couldn't come, though he wanted to. This was a very close family of three. The young boy was a leader at school and church, and gave the message one Sunday evening when the youth group was responsible for the service. The next Sunday morning he was overwhelmed with homosexual thoughts toward the pastor. The boy had such a good relationship with his parents that he told them about it. That was highly unusual, and it was just as unusual that the parents knew what to do about it. They recognized where those thoughts were coming from. They instructed their son not to pay any attention to them and to keep choosing the truth, which he did. By the time we met, the tempting thoughts had all but subsided. I asked the boy, "Did you want to think those thoughts, and did you make a conscious choice to do so?" Of course he didn't. The mother only wanted to know if there was anything else they needed to do.

Suppose a young boy is tempted by a sexual thought toward another boy at school. It is just a tempting thought, and it may have no impact at first. He knows nothing about taking every thought captive to the obedience of Christ, or finding a way of escape. Suppose he dwells on those thoughts, even though he may believe it is wrong at first, because he suspects it is abnormal. Thinking such thoughts will affect how he feels. That is the way God made us. So he starts wondering, *If I am thinking these thoughts, then I must be gay!* That process may take months or even years to unfold, but one day he believes the lie, and he acts upon it with another boy or man. Now he has used his body as an instrument of unrighteousness, and he has allowed sin to reign in his mortal body. Most young people will keep that hidden for years, but one day they will likely step out of the closet, announce they are gay, and walk away from their family and church. It is happening all around the world.

As I have shared that information around the country, many have talked with me afterward and shared that this is exactly what happened to them. A university professor said, "I have feared for years that I was gay. I have a good marriage and family. I can't tell you what this insight means to me." Two years later I was in the same area, and he came to help us minister to others. In the course of those two years he had helped over sixty men overcome their struggle with lust and homosexual tendencies.

In 1989, Marshal Kirk and Hunter Madsen published *After the Ball: How America Will Conquer Its Fear and Hatred of Gays in the '90s.* They laid out a plan for normalizing behavior that had previously been viewed as deviant: First, desensitize the citizen to deviancy by making deviancy appear positive. Second, make people feel guilty about their perceived bigotries, often equating homosexual and race bigotry. Third, through the media, display as normal that which had previously been viewed as abnormal. Some politicians in the United States have made the acceptance of homosexuality and same-sex marriage the next crusade for "civil rights." At the time of this writing the homosexual community has more political clout in the United States than the evangelical community.

Equating homosexuality as a civil rights agenda with the struggle for racial equality has infuriated conservative African American church leaders, as it should. It is not "politically correct" to present a biblical standard for sexuality, which makes the church look archaic to liberal progressivism. Freedom for the progressive is understood by Christians as license. For a good understanding of this cultural shift, I recommend *Sex and the iWorld* by Dale S. Kuehne.[2]

The number of Americans who are gay, lesbian, bisexual, or transgender is about nine million.[3] That constitutes about 3 percent of the population, which is not what the public hears. Any sect that makes up 3 percent of the population has little or no political clout, but a group of 10 percent or more does. I personally believe that the battle is less about homosexuality and more about personal "freedom," the casting off of social constraints, including any authoritative teaching from the Bible. Many people today will rush to the defense of anyone who is marginalized, excluded, rejected, or even frowned upon by what they perceive to be religious bigots, even if they disagree with the behavior of the one they are defending. The church has some culpability in this matter.

The "sciences" of secular psychology and psychiatry have stated their positions on homosexuality, which stand in stark contrast to the biblical standard of sexual morality. The official position of the American Psychological Association is that homosexuality is not a mental disorder, but rather a "normal aspect of human sexuality." It goes on to warn that conversion therapy is poorly documented and could cause potential harm.[4] The American Psychiatric Association adds, "There is no published scientific evidence supporting the efficacy of 'reparative therapy' as a treatment to change one's sexual orientation."[5]

There is now! Christian psychologists Stanton Jones and Mark Yarhouse have conducted research over several years. They tested the impact of ex-gay programs on participants—whether they actually experienced change, and whether the attempts to change caused additional stress. Their findings as of this writing have contradicted the established professional consensus, which they report in their book *Ex-Gays? A Longitudinal Study of Religiously Mediated Change in Sexual Orientation.*[6] That will not silence the opposition to the biblical standard of sexuality, however, because they will argue that their sample was too small. No study conducted by Christian researchers would be large enough to sway our culture, because this isn't a scientific or a political issue. It is a moral and spiritual issue.

God created us male and female. So clear is that distinction that one's sexual identity can be determined by a DNA sample. Our bodies are telling the truth. It was the soul that got damaged and that can be repaired. God did not create anyone to be a homosexual, and the Israelites were commanded under the Law to maintain that distinction. "A woman must not wear men's clothing, nor a man wear women's clothing, for the Lord your God detests anyone who does this" (Deuteronomy 22:5). Homosexual "marriages" and sexual relations were also clearly forbidden: "Do not lie with a man as one lies with a woman; that is detestable" (Leviticus 18:22), and even stronger words are recorded in 20:13: "If a man lies with a man as one lies with a woman, both of them have done what is detestable. They must be put to death; their blood will be on their own heads." Obviously the latter is no longer an option, unless you live under Islamic law. It is important to note that adultery was also a capital offense under the Law, and the church should hold it as equally wrong.

Some may argue that we are no longer under the Law, and therefore not subject to it. Jesus did not come to abolish the Law, but to fulfill it. The moral standards of God have not changed. "Do not be deceived: Neither the sexually immoral nor adulterers nor male prostitutes nor homosexual offenders nor thieves nor the greedy nor drunkards nor slanderers nor swindlers will inherit the kingdom of God" (1 Corinthians 6:9–10). Notice that sexual sins were the first four mentioned in the rogues' gallery.

We are called to make disciples and to be ambassadors for Christ. Christ looked upon the multitude with compassion, and so must we. Those who refuse to believe and repent have a sure destiny of eternal separation from God, which should cause us to weep. Their sin has separated them from God, and we must be available to give an answer for the hope that lies within us. How they happen to manifest their sin is not the problem. It is just the evidence that they are separated from God. They need the Lord, and it is our responsibility to offer them the gospel, which includes forgiveness and new life in Christ. After the apostle Paul's scathing indictment of the aberrant behavior mentioned above, he wrote of authentic transformation, saying, "Such were some of you; but you were washed, but you were sanctified, but you were justified in the name of the Lord Jesus Christ and in the Spirit of our God" (1 Corinthians 6:11 NASB). We have the opportunity to bring a message of hope, but it must be given with grace and compassion. We cannot teach the good news and be the bad news.

Tragically, the public perception of the conservative church's stance on homosexuality has appeared more condemning than redemptive. In many cases we have prohibited certain behaviors, but not provided an adequate answer for those who wish to be rightly related to God. Condemning the behavior without giving them some hope for overcoming sexual strongholds has caused many to reject the church.

Those who are struggling with same-sex attraction fall into three categories: First, there are the militant gays who flaunt their sexual desires. They march in parades espousing gay pride. They don't like the church, and are generally resistant to the gospel no matter how it is shared. Second, there are those who want to continue in their sexual orientation, but prefer to remain in the closet. They want to appear as respectable members of society. The first group wants this second group to come out and will put pressure on them to do so. Third, there are those who feel shameful about their orientation, and many of them come to our churches hoping that we have an answer. While the first group may viciously slander Christianity, the second group will likely ignore us.

Suppose someone in the third category is attending your church, and he or she hears you correctly teach God's moral standard for sex. How do you think the person would feel? Ashamed? Condemned? Not many are likely to come forward and admit their struggle. So they remain silent and hope none will find out what they are struggling with. Couple that with the fact that a large majority of those who struggle with homosexual tendencies have been sexually abused. The last thing we want to do is add more abuse. I have a lot more empathy for someone who is caught in this struggle than I do for the heterosexual person who cheated on his or her spouse.

Although the church has made serious errors in the past, we cannot compromise our commitment to the authority of God's Word. Such people can't be right with God if He said their behavior is an abomination to Him. If we truly care for another person's relationship with God, then we have to help them remove the barriers to their intimacy with God through genuine repentance and faith.

God did not create people to be homosexuals or alcoholics. Because of the fall, however, we can be genetically predisposed to certain strengths and weaknesses—but that doesn't make anyone a homosexual or an alcoholic. No attempt has been made to explain why others who have a similar genetic predisposition aren't struggling with homosexuality or alcoholism. There is no demon of homosexuality zapping people with that affliction. Such simplistic thinking has harmed the reputation of the church. On the other hand, there is clearly a spiritual battle for the mind that can result in sexual immorality when yielded to.

In Romans 1:18–32, the apostle Paul explained our descent into sexual immorality. In summary, God has made himself known in such a way that all are without excuse. For those who don't believe, God gave them up in the lusts of their hearts to impurity, dishonoring their bodies because they exchanged the truth about God for a lie. They worshiped and served the creature rather than the Creator. They didn't repent, so God gave them up to dishonorable passions, and they exchanged natural relations for those that are contrary to nature. Women burned in lust for other women, and men burned in lust for other men. They still didn't honor God, so He gave them up to a debased mind to do what ought not to be done. A reprobate or depraved mind is no longer capable of sound judgment. Such people are filled with all manner of unrighteousness, evil, covetousness, and malice. As a nation, we are clearly between the second and the third stage and looking more and more like the decline of the Roman Empire, which took the same course.

Our ministry is to equip the church to help those who want to live a righteous life. This must begin with a spiritual check on our own biases. As repugnant as deviant sex may be from our perspective, we have to "dine with sinners" as Jesus did. By that I mean we have to love the inquirer and set aside how bad we hate the sin. If we can't conceal our repugnance, then we need to step aside and let someone else be the encourager. Love covers a multitude of sins.

Finding an intimate relationship with God will, hopefully, enable those who are coming out of that lifestyle to establish new healthy relationships with other believers. Such people are not gay Christians. The Bible never refers to believers by their flesh patterns, or by who they were "in Adam." Being part of a loving and supportive community of believers is essential for complete recovery. It takes time to overcome a distorted self-perception and grow in the grace of God. Unfortunately, homosexuality has become the new leprosy for some conservative churches. We want to keep ourselves, our spouses, and our children away from such deviant behavior. This may be one of the biggest challenges we face. The goal is to become like Christ, and not be like the Pharisees.

Patience is a virtue that must be cultivated when working with those who are struggling with addictive behaviors. Salvation pulls victims out of the swamp, but they are often covered with leeches, mud, and other creepy things, which may cause some to shy away. Such attachments will slowly fall off as they mature. The church must offer them acceptance and guidance, because they may lose heart and return to the swamp. We can offer them Christ, but if we don't offer them a friend, we will likely lose them, which is true for every new believer. If we draw near to the throne of grace, we will receive mercy and find grace to help in the time of need (see Hebrews 4:16). That is what we must offer those who desire to overcome addictive behaviors and live a righteous life.

"If you had the chance to overcome sexual strongholds and be free from the past without public embarrassment, would you take it?" I wrote that on the back cover of *Winning the Battle Within.* I have no desire to expose anyone's sin, which is why I wrote the book so that no one has to share anything intimate unless they so desire. The questions at the end of each chapter are for discussion about the truth and don't ask for personal disclosure. The Steps to Freedom in Christ are included in the book. If you are leading an individual or group through the study, you can finish by leading them through the Steps, giving them the opportunity to have their own encounter with God. If we don't offer them that opportunity, very few people are going to come forward to seek help—unless they are caught in the act of sin. A disciple-making church gives believers the chance to overcome the guilt and shame of sexual strongholds.

NINE
Overcoming Chemical Addictions

A seminary student walked into my office and slowly closed the door. "I'm dropping out of seminary," he said. His eyes never left the floor as he stood nervously in front of me, waiting for my response. Not everybody makes it through seminary, so this wasn't totally out of the ordinary. He was a decent student, but he had missed a few classes.

"Why are you leaving?" I asked. The fidgeting became more noticeable before he finally responded, "I guess I'm an alcoholic." "So why are you dropping out?" I asked. I think he was a little surprised by my response. Most people struggling with addictive behaviors in Christian circles fear the possibility of being "found out," and they expect the hammer to fall when

This chapter is adapted from *Overcoming Addictive Behavior*, which I coauthored with Mike Quarles. Mike was a stockbroker who found Christ while recovering from alcoholism. He became a Presbyterian pastor, but resigned when he realized that what he was teaching wasn't working for him. He fell back into alcoholism and was at the absolute bottom when he discovered who he was in Christ. He never drank again, and together we wrote *Freedom From Addiction*, in which he shared his story.

they are. We had a long talk that afternoon, and we worked together to draft a plan for his recovery. Fortunately, he had a good pastor who I knew would work with us to help him break free from his addiction.

One of the more meaningful graduations that I ever suffered through as a seminary professor came two years later when this young man walked across the platform and received his diploma, two years sober. It may be a little unusual for a seminary student to be hooked on alcohol, but it is not unusual to find this problem in our churches or in Christian ministries.

There are more than twenty million alcoholics in the United States, 25 percent of which are teens and young adults. Of those who claim to be social drinkers, one in ten is an alcoholic. The ratio is one in three if they attend a Bible-believing church. Christians are more likely to be secretive about their drinking, which is counterproductive to their Christian walk as well as their recovery in Christ. With the proliferation of Native American gaming and state-run lotteries, there are more people addicted to gambling than to alcohol and drugs. In many evangelical churches, it isn't socially acceptable to drink excessively or to gamble, so we opt for a more socially acceptable way of dealing with stress. We turn to food, our drug of choice, and call it fellowship. Casting our anxieties upon the refrigerator will not be healthy in the end (pardon the pun).

Consider Nancy, who is fifty years old and exhibits many maladaptive psychological, physical, and spiritual symptoms. She feels lethargic about life, struggles with interpersonal relationships at home, and doesn't seem to connect at church. She makes an appointment to see her doctor, who discovers that her blood sugar levels are high, precipitated by her secret habit of drinking alcohol. In spite of the fact that Nancy is at least seventy-five pounds overweight, the doctor doesn't question her about her eating habits or lack of exercise. Her spiritual condition isn't considered as an option for treatment, so the doctor gives Nancy a written prescription for an oral diabetes medication to treat her prediabetic symptoms.

Nancy dutifully takes her medication and makes an appointment to see her pastor. He listens patiently about her struggle with depression and family problems. He asks about her prayer and devotional life, which are virtually nonexistent. He suggests that she spend more time with God on a daily basis and recommends a good book to partially replace her television "addiction." Meanwhile, she continues her same eating habits and makes a halfhearted attempt to improve her spiritual disciplines.

The medication for her prediabetic condition gives her chronic indigestion, so she starts taking an H_2 blocker like Tagamet, which reduces her digestive symptoms, but now her stomach acid, which was low to begin with, is practically nonexistent. Consequently, she's not digesting food as well, which reduces her nutritional input. The medication also puts more stress on her kidneys, and with her estrogen level low, she gets a urinary tract infection.

Her doctor puts Nancy on antibiotics for the infection, but that lowers her immune system and kills most of the beneficial bacteria in her colon. The result is a bad case of the flu, which she can't seem to overcome, and she has constant gas from a colon imbalance.

She starts taking antihistamines for a sinus infection, and her doctor recommends a hysterectomy to solve her recurrent urinary tract infections. Nancy has the surgery and starts taking synthetic hormones, which make her feel depressed and weepy. She sees a psychiatrist, who prescribes an antidepressant. Nancy is now taking a diabetic medicine, an H_2 blocker, antihistamines, synthetic hormones, an antidepressant, and a shot of gin when she needs it. She's exhausted all the time, mentally flaky, emotionally withdrawn, and waiting for the next health problem to hit, which it will!

Let's start over again. Instead of seeing her doctor, Nancy decides to confide with a trained encourager at her church. After hearing her story, the encourager senses that Nancy has some unresolved personal and spiritual issues and invites her to attend a small group that is going to start the Freedom in Christ discipleship course. Nancy's inclination is to decline the offer, because another night out sounds like too much work for someone so exhausted. The encourager reminds her that it would be good to get away from family responsibilities once a week and do something for herself for a change.

Reluctantly, she agrees to attend the class. The encourager recognizes that Nancy needs a lifestyle change and invites Nancy to come with her to the YMCA and start an exercise program that isn't too extreme. She meets a new friend at the Freedom in Christ class who shares how she lost several pounds just by eating smarter. They agree to meet and discuss proper nutrition.

Several months later, Nancy has found her freedom in Christ and discovered what it means to be a child of God. With the encouragement of her friend, she has stuck it out at the Y and her energy level has increased significantly, due partly to her new eating habits. She has lost twenty pounds, and her blood sugar level is normal. She has made some new friends at the Y and at the small-group Bible study. This isn't rocket science. It is biblically informed common sense.

Obesity is considered the number one health problem in America. Every year we hear of a new revolutionary diet program, but people continue to put on the pounds. There is one common thread through every diet program and every secular recovery program. They are all based on the concept of law. There is something you must abstain from, or something you must do.

A newspaper article featured a woman who was commissioned by her state's board of education to lecture students on the subject of safe sex. The assumption was, if students only knew the dangers of sexually transmitted diseases, they would behave properly. The woman had a major weight problem. Consequently, she had devoured books on nutrition, exercise, and diet. She probably knew enough to give lectures on those subjects as well, but knowing all that information didn't stop her from having a second piece of pie before her first presentation. How honest and insightful! She realized from her own experience that telling people what they are doing is wrong does not give them the power to stop doing it. If that approach didn't work for her as an adult, how could she expect it to work for children?

For years the U.S. government ran the D.A.R.E. program with the slogan "Just say no!" Did that work? No! Laying down the law doesn't work in the church either. Paul argued that the law has the capacity to stimulate the desire to do what it had intended to prohibit (see Romans 7:5, 8). If you don't think that is true, try telling a child that he can't go there, but he can go here. The moment you say that, where does he want to go? God said Adam and Eve could eat from any tree in the garden, except for that one tree. Which one was Eve tempted to eat from? We are "servants of a new covenant, not of the letter but of the Spirit; for the letter kills, but the Spirit gives life" (2 Corinthians 3:6).

The popular twelve-step program to overcome addiction began with the Oxford Group, which originally proposed six steps. It was a Christ-centered Presbyterian program that showed good results. Others took note and wanted to use the program, but they didn't want to embrace Christ. Six more steps were added and the concept of God was replaced by a higher power, and it ceased being a Christian ministry.

The turbulent sixties surfaced a number of Christians needing help to overcome addictive behaviors, and the church responded. Just like we tried to "Christianize" secular psychology, we tried to "Christianize" secular recovery programs, and with the programs came a lot of beliefs that aren't consistent with Scripture and sanctified common sense. Let me name a few.

First, they instruct participants to work the program, because the program works. There is no program that can set anyone free. That is a law-based concept. The reason the original six steps worked was because of Christ, not because of the program.

Second, they teach that alcoholism is a disease and incurable. Once you are an alcoholic, you will always be an alcoholic. That is bad theology that sounds like "Once a sinner, always a sinner." That is not true either. Once we were sinners, but now we are saints who sin. You can't expect to live a righteous life if your core identity is still sin. Calling addiction a disease is supposed to make them feel better, but it may also absolve some from assuming their responsibility to live a righteous life: "It's not my fault. I have this disease!" Sin is not a disease. The medical profession is now saying that obesity is a disease. I first heard that on the news when they paraded an obese, theologically liberal pastor before the camera who thought that was progress. Sin is what separates us from God when we are sinners, and sin is what keeps us from an intimate relationship with Him when we become His children.

Third, they introduce themselves as addicts, alcoholics, co-addicts, and co-alcoholics. Shouldn't the Christian say, "Hi, I'm Neil, I'm a child of God who is struggling with a certain flesh pattern, but I am learning how to overcome my addiction by the grace of God"? Reinforcing a failure identity is counterproductive to becoming complete in Christ. Paul never identifies a believer by their flesh patterns. "Therefore from now on we recognize no one according to their flesh" (2 Corinthians 5:16).

Fourth, their goal is sobriety. If abstinence is the goal, then Ephesians 5:18 would read, "Be not drunk with wine, therefore stop drinking." The apostle Paul has a different answer, "Be filled with the Spirit." "But I say, walk by the Spirit, and you will not carry out the desire of the flesh" (Galatians 5:16). What happens if you take alcohol away from someone addicted to it? You have a dry drunk, and the person will likely be more miserable than they were before. Plus, you just took away their means of coping without giving them a better way. That is why 97 percent will return to their drug of choice within weeks and months after leaving a thirty-day treatment center. Have you ever tried to take an old bone away from a dog? You will have a dog fight. Try throwing him a steak, and he will be a lot more willing to spit out the old bone.

Fifth, they talk about dual diagnosis, but the reality is multiple diagnosis. Show me anyone who is addicted to anything, and I will show you someone who has a poor sense of worth, who is depressed, anxious, fearful, ashamed, angry, and bitter. Do you think they can resolve all that plus their relational problems at home by simply taking away their drug of choice? Additionally, the vast majority of people who are seeking treatment for chemical addiction are also sexually addicted, and in most cases that is not even addressed. They also know that sexual addictions are harder to overcome than chemical addictions, and much easier to cover up.

Finally, if you attend one of these self-help groups, you will hear phrases like "You have to get rid of that stinking thinking," or "Don't pay attention to that 'committee' in your head." Most recovery programs are not taking into account the reality of the spiritual world, and don't acknowledge or understand the spiritual battle going on for their minds. Have you ever tried to not think sexual thoughts or tempting thoughts? Did that work?

People abuse chemicals for three basic reasons. The first is peer-pressure-induced "party time." To have a good time they have to get rid of their inhibitions. Everybody is doing it, and you don't want to be the party pooper! The nerd! The odd person out! The first puff on a cigarette, the first taste of beer, and the first sip of hard liquor is seldom, if ever, a good experience. So why do so many people proceed with an act that their natural senses reject? Very few young people are secure enough in their faith to stand alone when everyone else at school, work, or play is drinking and using. They have a better chance if they have a Christian support group—which will probably be far less popular—that will accept them for who they are and provide them a sense of belonging.

Second, some turn to chemicals to escape the pressures of life. That is what happy hour is all about. *I'll just stop off after work and have a couple of drinks, and maybe one for the road.* Our emotional development is arrested the moment we turn to chemicals to reduce our stress and cope with the pressures of living. Popping pills to mask the anxiety of a troubled marriage or dysfunctional family can only lead to disaster. Taking meds of any kind is the cultural norm for silencing a troubled mind.

My attempt to help a couple was leading nowhere. The husband was struggling at work, home, and church. Everyone was wrong except him. I didn't see either of them for months. Then one evening out of the blue, I got a call from him. He had just been released from jail after three months, and I was the first one he called. He said, "This is the first time that I have been clean in ten years." I had no idea that he had been abusing drugs. I don't think his wife knew. He told me that he sold just enough drugs at work to feed his addiction. I asked him, "Knowing that you were on the verge of losing your job, your wife, and even your church, why did you continue to use?" He said, "That was the only time that I ever felt good about myself." I have never forgotten that statement, because of what it did for me. I went from wanting to strangle him to wishing he were present so I could hug him. How much more could I have helped him if I'd understood that?

Third, people turn to medications to stop the pain. That is the major reason why people abuse prescription medications. If you have a banging toothache, you don't care about politics, other people, or world evangelization. You only want to stop the pain, and that pain is often more emotional than physical.

The Cycle of Addiction

There are many paths to addiction, but the cycle that spirals downward is similar for all those caught in the web of dependency. Please refer to the chart on the following page as I discuss the addiction cycle for alcoholics. The "baseline experience" refers to the mental and emotional state that people experience when they first begin to use drugs or drink or gamble or encounter their first sexual stimulation. The first drink, puff, snort, or sexual titillation brings an immediate onset of chemical reaction in the body—a rush. Alcohol and drugs don't step on the accelerator; they release the brake. There is a feeling of euphoria from the effect of the chemicals or from the touch of a girl or from a slot machine payoff. Getting high can be fun for the moment.

The baseline experience is different for those who are looking for a temporary reprieve from the pressures of life. Such people could be a bundle of nerves or depressed about their circumstances. They are looking for a high to lift their spirits or something to calm their nerves. Melancholy people just want to drown their sorrows. Alcohol or drugs will help them mellow out. It works! Within a matter of minutes they feel better. The same is true for those who want to stop the pain. They can't wait for that rush to take effect. When it does, they will feel better.

The Addiction Cycle

Euphoria
(Mellowed Out)

Rush
(Onset of
Reaction)

Addiction:
1. Habituation
2. Dependency
3. Tolerance
4. Withdrawal

Baseline Experience

Guilt

Fear

Shame

Grandiose, aggressive behavior

Efforts to control fail repeatedly

Tries geographical escapes

Family and friends avoided

Loss of ordinary willpower

Tremors and early morning drinks

Decrease in ability to stop drinking

Onset of lengthy intoxication

Moral deterioration

Impaired thinking

Drink with inferiors

Unable to initiate actions

Obsession with drinking

All alibis exhausted

Occasional drinking

Increase in tolerance

Memory blacks out

Excuses increase

Surreptitious drinking

Increased dependency

Persistent remorse

Promises fail

Loss of interest

Work, money troubles

Resentments pile up

Neglect of food

Physical deterioration

Irrational fears

Obsessions

Physical illness

Complete defeat

Death or recovery

Unfortunately, the effect wears off. The morning after is a different story. Addicts wake up feeling just a little bit lower than they did at their baseline experience. Reality sets in, and the head aches. They hardly recognize the person in the mirror. At work or school, all the pressures and responsibilities of life come rushing back. There could be twinges of guilt, shame, or fear, depending upon the person's conscience. For some it could be a complete violation of everything they have ever been taught and believed. It was a bad experience, and they promise to never put themselves in a position of compromise again.

On the other hand, it was kind of fun. For the party animal, it was a great experience, and they can hardly wait to do it again. They never had so much fun. They live from weekend to weekend, from party to party. They live for the euphoria. They get a rush just thinking about it.

The first step toward addiction is habituation. This pattern of behavior becomes the means to have a good time or to cope with life. A habit is a knee-jerk response. A flesh pattern. You feel a pain, so you reach for the pills. You feel down, so you do something that will pick you up. You feel stressed out, so you do something that will calm your nerves. It worked before, so it will work again. You have trained yourself to depend upon something to pick you up, to stop the pain, to soothe your nerves, to make you feel good. You don't believe that you can have a good time or feel good without it. Occasional drinking, gambling, sexual titillation, or using drugs has become a habit, a means of emotional support, a crutch to lean on.

When the effects wear off, the guilt, fear, and shame become more and more pronounced. With each successive use the addict gets further and further away from the original baseline experience. Feeling like the king of the hill when they are high, addicts are filled with grandiose ideas and many become more aggressive in their behavior. They feel emboldened. On the downside, alcoholics and addicts begin to experience memory blackouts, and efforts to regain control of their lives fail repeatedly. *How did I get home last night? What happened? I better get a grip on myself—I'm starting to lose control!* Most alcoholics feel guilty about their behavior, so they begin to drink surreptitiously, and they leave familiar surroundings to go where people don't know them. They can't live with the shame.

Initially, all they want is to reach that elusive high they once felt and experience the euphoria once more. The problem is it takes more and more alcohol and a greater fix to reach that original high. Every user develops a tolerance for their drug of choice—and the same happens with people addicted to sex. It may have taken two beers when they first started, now it takes a case. Then beer is too slow, and a chaser is needed to speed up the process. Marijuana was fine at first, but now it takes cocaine. Aspirin used to stop the headache; now it barely has an impact. The first kiss was exciting, and that led to petting, but now that isn't enough. Alcoholics and addicts will never experience the euphoria they once did, no matter how much they drink or take. As the lows get lower, so do the potential highs. Before long all they hope for is to get back to their baseline experience, but even that begins to elude them. They are the prodigal sons who would rather go back home and be a hired man for their father, not realizing their Father would welcome them as His children.

A loss of willpower robs addicts of their ability to live a responsible life at home and eventually at work. The cost to support their habit almost always causes severe financial problems. Many white-collar workers may be able to support their habit for years and carry on their masquerade in public, but their family will suffer tremendous hardship. The poor will steal and become pushers to support their addiction. The morality of both will deteriorate.

Addicts have no sense of worth, nor any self-respect. They are disgusted with themselves. They don't eat well and don't take care of themselves. Consequently, their physical health becomes a factor.

Those who have a reputation to uphold and suffer from a chemical addiction will start to withdraw from social contacts. They don't want their weaknesses to be seen or known, and they fear being publicly humiliated or exposed. They become paranoid about others looking at them or talking about them. They have no mental peace. Condemning voices haunt them day and night. *You're disgusting. Why don't you just check out? You're good for nothing. Your family would be better off without you.* The only way they know how to silence those voices is to keep drinking.

Intervention

I don't have a drinking problem. I can stop any time. The only way to prove that is to stop. Unfortunately, many have to lose their job, family, and health before they will admit to their addiction. It is the same pride that keeps pagans from admitting their need for a Savior and Christians from admitting their need for a Lord. Brokenness is the key to any recovery ministry. God will orchestrate that process if we don't take the initiative ourselves. He did for me! "Therefore humble yourselves under the mighty hand of God, that He may exalt you at the proper time" (1 Peter 5:6).

When we see others on a downward spiral, it is possible to take the initiative and schedule an intervention. It will be more effective if experienced and unbiased or outside help is solicited, because family members have often been too judgmental and condemning, or too busy covering up and pretending that all is well. An intervention gathers all the principle people (including the boss at work if applicable) in the alcoholic's or addict's life in a well-orchestrated time of confrontation. Some will rehearse the intervention without the alcoholic's knowledge. It should be scheduled at a time when he or she is sober. Each person then relates what the alcoholic's addiction is doing to them personally. The alcoholic or addict is then given an opportunity to seek treatment, which has already been arranged. Speaking the truth in love and holding ground are the two most vital ingredients to get addicts to seek the help they need.

Codependent No More

The downward spiral that all addicts find themselves in is like a tornado that gathers up victims in its path and hurls them out of the way. The primary victims are the other family members. The spouse is the first affected. When I was pastoring a church, a faithful attendee and worker in the church made an appointment to see me. I hardly knew her husband because he was seldom seen with her at church. His wife had often requested prayer for his salvation, but she never shared the family secret. Twenty years of silence were broken that afternoon. She couldn't live that way any longer. His alcoholism had destroyed their family and their marriage.

For twenty years she was the classic enabler. If he couldn't make it to work because of his drinking, she covered for him. If he passed out drunk on the front lawn, she would somehow get him in the house, clean him up, and put him to bed. The children were told to do the same. They had to protect the family name and make sure the chief breadwinner didn't lose his job. Lying and covering up became the means of survival. Family members were threatened if they didn't play along, and even if they did play the game, they still suffered mentally, emotionally, and physically. The shame they bore kept them locked in silence.

Enablers have learned to cope and survive by lying and covering up. The fear of retaliation keeps them silent. Their identity and sense of worth is shattered by what is happening at home. They believe they will lose their last shred of dignity by blowing the whistle. Some people would blame them for breaking up the family, which unfortunately happens in many abuse cases. The biblical mandates to "speak the truth in love" (see Ephesians 4:15) and "walk in the Light" (1 John 1:7) are abandoned for self-preservation. But just the opposite is happening—self-destruction. They are in bondage to their own lies and bitterness.

If someone is traveling down a road to destruction, do you want to enable the process? You will never help the addict or the abuser by enabling them to continue in their irresponsible and immoral behavior. It will only get worse for both of you and undermine your relationship with God.

I say turn them in—to the boss, to the church, and even to the police if necessary. I say that not because I don't care, but because I do. The addict is like a misbehaving child screaming for attention, "Doesn't anybody care enough about me to stop me from destroying myself?" Discipline is a proof of our love, not a violation of it. The fear of being exposed is worse than the actual consequences of getting exposed. Most addicts are tired of living a lie, and many are relieved when they are finally caught. The consequences of doing nothing are worse than the consequences of taking a stand for everybody's sake.

Where Do We Start?

Many years ago I was invited to speak at the Rescue Mission in Los Angeles. It was not the noon or evening evangelistic meeting. I was speaking to the men who had made a decision for Christ and were in the discipleship program. When I walked in, they all stood and applauded. I thought Billy Graham or some other prominent person had followed me in. Actually, they weren't applauding me. They were acknowledging what I stood for. I learned later that they had been watching the DVD of the Freedom in Christ course. What they were applauding was the message I was going to share that morning, which they had already heard on the DVD.

I began, "Gentlemen, I want you to know that you are not a derelict, a bum, a drunk, an alcoholic, or an addict. You are children of God, and no, you have not committed the unpardonable sin." The place erupted again.

Most churches are not large enough to have a fully functioning recovery ministry, but that is not keeping them from being disciple-making churches. What every church can offer is an opportunity for addicts to repent and find their identity and freedom in Christ. If that is successful, then almost any program will work. However, a well-thought-out, biblically based program staffed by trained encouragers will bear more fruit than a poorly thought out program staffed by novices. Unfortunately, dedicated incompetency is still incompetency.

For an elective that I taught at Talbot School of Theology, I required students to attend an Alcoholics Anonymous (AA) meeting and give a report of their experience. Most struggled with the cigarette smoke and foul language, but almost everyone said, "I wish I could get my class or small group at church to be that honest." Most AA participants have already had their sins exposed, so there is nothing to cover up. I have no problem recommending the services of AA. Their twelve steps can be understood from a Christian perspective, and they know a lot about addiction. They have saved a lot of natural lives and provided the necessary support to start again. It is not what Christian AA groups are offering that I struggle with; it is what they are not offering, which is a liberated life in Christ. Your church can offer that.

TEN

Setting Marriages Free

In the entire history of the church there has never been so much effort made by the Christian community to save the family as we have seen in recent years. Focus on the Family is by far the largest Christian radio ministry ever. Degreed programs on marriage and family ministries have sprung up all over the country. Books and videos addressing marriage and family issues are consistently big sellers. Saving marriages and families may be the greatest felt need of our time.

However, we need to ask a hard question: With all of these resources, how are we doing? Has the family as a whole become stronger in the United States and around the world? Have our marriages become better? Certainly we can point to the cultural revolution plaguing the world as a contributing factor, but have we missed something? I believe in most cases the Christian message has been biblically based, or at least consistent with what the Bible teaches about marriage and parenting. There are many excellent biblical resources available for the following family disciplines:

Each discipline is like a spoke that shapes and reinforces the Christian family. The wheel doesn't roll very well if it is out of balance. Focusing on the marital relationship while overlooking the needs of the children can throw the family out of balance, but the opposite is more likely to happen. Also, the family and marriage will not be very strong if spokes are missing—such as consistent discipline or communication. Most churches have addressed these issues from the pulpit and classrooms, and let's assume the presentations have been biblically accurate. So why isn't it more effective? The divorce rate for Christians is just slightly less than that of the world.

A doctor in a church I pastored told me that he and his wife were having marriage problems. So he arranged for them to attend a weekend marriage retreat taught by a well-known and highly respected Christian author. He said, "The content was excellent, but we argued all the way there and all the way back."

It isn't intentional, but biblical instruction can be a subtle form of Christian behaviorism—i.e., trying to change behavior without changing the person. "You shouldn't do that. You should do this, or here is a better way to do it." That may not be legalism in a pharisaic sense, but in some cases the emphasis has shifted from negative legalism (don't do this and don't do that) to "positive" legalism (do this, do this, do this, and do this, ad nauseam). Actually, there is nothing positive about legalism, regardless of its emphasis. When applied to marriage, such counsel sounds like this:

> Mr. Jones, have you loved your wife as Christ loved the church? Would you be willing to if you knew how? Let me suggest some practical ways that you could do that, and possibly some behaviors and words that would be best left undone and unsaid.
>
> Mrs. Jones, have you respected your husband as the head of your home? My wife would be happy to share with you what she has learned after years of living with me.
>
> Do you suppose you both could do those things for each other? Good! I'm going to give you an exercise on marital communication that I would like you to work through this week. Let's meet again next week at this same time and see how you are doing.

Pointing out our biblical roles and responsibilities and suggesting how to accomplish them may be appropriate in the right circumstances. However, trying to get people to behave more appropriately as a couple when each is torn up on the inside will not work. That would be like two people trying to dance when one or both are on crutches. How can they become one in Christ if neither is experiencing their freedom in Christ?

What is missing in the previous diagram is Christ. It should look like this:

A Christian marriage is a spiritual union with God that is intended to be a visible expression of the relationship that God has with the church, which is the bride of Christ. Notice how they are intertwined in Ephesians 5:25–28 (NIV1984):

> Husbands, love your wives, just as Christ loved the church and gave himself up for her to make her holy, cleansing her by the washing with water through the word, and to present her to himself as a radiant church, without stain or wrinkle or any other blemish, but holy and blameless. In this same way, husbands ought to love their wives as their own bodies.

We cannot do in the flesh what God by His power can do through us. What makes this so subtle is that all the spokes in the wheel could be soundly biblical and yet not be connected to the hub. In most cases it is not what we are doing wrong. It is more a case of what is missing. It is like a new car trying to fulfill its purpose when it is out of gas. Of course we want people to behave according to God's standards, but they never will if they are trying to live by godly principles in their own strength. To bear fruit we have to be connected to the source of life.

We can't bear fruit without abiding in Christ. Bearing fruit is the evidence that we are abiding in Christ. "I am the vine; you are the branches. If a man remains [abides] in me and I in him, he will bear much fruit; apart from me you can do nothing" (John 15:5 NIV1984). Without Christ we are not just handicapped or limited in what we can do; without Christ we cannot do anything of eternal significance! We are incomplete without Him, and our marriages are as well. To maintain a Christian marriage, we have to become one "in Christ." Just saying that won't change anything. It has to be individually appropriated through repentance and faith. If you have a church full of people in the bondage of bitterness or other unresolved conflicts, you have a church full of bad marriages. If you have a church full of bad marriages, you have a bad church. The whole cannot be greater than the sum of its parts.

There are scriptural passages that relate to marriage and family in the Old Testament and in the second half of Paul's epistles, which are generally divided into two sections. Many have observed that the first half of Paul's epistles are more theological, and the second half are more practical. Those who focus on marriage and family ministries concentrate their time on the practical aspects of Christian living, which are in the second half of Paul's epistles. I firmly believe that if we can help people enter into the first half of Paul's epistles, which establishes them in Christ, they will be able to live out the second half supernaturally.

Can we expect men to behave like Christian husbands when they don't have a clue who they are in Christ or what it means to be a child of God? Can we expect women who are plagued by many unresolved personal and spiritual conflicts to behave like Christian wives? To put it bluntly, my advice to struggling couples often sounds like this: *Forget your marriage; you are so torn up on the inside that you probably couldn't get along with your dog right now. But if you are willing to resolve your own personal and spiritual conflicts first and get radically right with God, then there is great hope for your marriage.*

A pastor asked if I would counsel a couple on his staff. This was their last chance. If I couldn't help them, the pastor would dismiss him, and that would likely lead to a divorce. They were like two armadillos with their tails tied together heading in opposite directions, and the knot was slipping. Both were defending themselves against the other's propensity to claw.

I told them to forget their marriage. There was no way that any words of mine would change their relationship. I asked the wife if she had a place to get away for a couple of weeks. She said she did. Her family had a cabin nearby. I gave her a set of recordings that would help her understand who she is in Christ and how she could resolve the bitterness and pain she was experiencing. I encouraged the husband to do the same at home. I asked them not to work through the material for the purpose of saving their marriage, but rather for the sole purpose of finding their own identity and freedom in Christ. I even suggested they shouldn't talk to each other for two weeks. To my surprise, they agreed. Frankly, I didn't hold out much hope for them.

I didn't see or hear from the couple for three years. Then one Sunday after church I was at a restaurant with my family. I saw the husband with his three children, but no wife. Then, to my surprise, she came in and sat with her husband and children. She had been parking the car. After recognizing me, they shared what happened. They had actually taken my advice. Each had their own encounter with God, and each found their freedom in Christ. It was their individual connections to God that saved their marriage.

I have seen that happen numerous times with couples going through the Freedom in Christ course. Marriage is hardly even mentioned, and yet I have seen previously troubled couples walk out hand in hand after discovering their own identity and freedom in Christ. Hundreds of people have told me that I saved their marriage. Most were people I didn't even know, approaching me or writing to me in response to having read *Victory Over the Darkness* and *The Bondage Breaker*, which only allude to the subject of marriage.

We can have a house full of Christians and not have a Christian home. If just one member of the family has a root of bitterness, the whole family can be defiled. The other members of the family sense the tension in the home and either work together to heal the wounds or drift apart, seeking peace in isolation. Have you ever noticed that when the spiritual tide is out, all the little tadpoles want to swim in their own little tide pool? But when the spiritual tide is in, they all swim harmoniously together as though somebody other than themselves is orchestrating every move. To have a Christian home, it must begin with marital reconciliation.

Steps to Setting Your Marriage Free

Being fully reconciled to God is what makes it possible to be reconciled with one another. Trying to unite fallen humanity on any basis other than Christ has always failed. We are to be merciful to others as God has been merciful to us. We forgive others as God has forgiven us. We love because we have first been loved. A ministry of reconciliation must always begin with God. If that is successful, then we are free to give to others what God has freely given to us.

Using the same premise that makes the individual's Steps to Freedom so effective (namely, the inclusion of God through prayer), Chuck Mylander and I developed the Steps to Setting Your Marriage Free. Essentially, it is a corporate repentance process that is dependent upon the presence of God. He is the One who grants repentance. It begins with a prayer of commitment by husband and wife. Then each step begins with the couple praying together, asking the Lord to guide them. Each spouse sits silently before the Lord and individually works on their own issues. The one absolute rule is that each spouse must deal with his or her own issues, and cannot deal with the spouse's issues. For some that is a very hard rule to follow. In other words, they cannot play the role of the Holy Spirit in the other person's life. The process breaks down if one will not assume responsibility for their own attitudes and actions. In such cases we have a modified version of the Steps to Setting Your Marriage Free that the responsible husband or wife can process on his or her own. Nobody is keeping the responsible spouse from being the husband or wife that God created them to be. Assuming one's own responsibility preserves their intimate relationship with God, and that is the best way to save the marriage in the future.

After both spouses have dealt with their own individual issues before God, they are invited to come back together and share with one another. Usually that includes some confession and asking the other for forgiveness. Then they begin the Steps:

Step One: Establish God's Priority for Marriage. In what ways has either spouse not left their parents—physically, spiritually, mentally, emotionally, and financially? Many well-intentioned, and not so well-intentioned, parents have ruined the marriages of their children. Some newlyweds are still dependent upon their parents instead of on God and each other.

Step Two: Break Cycles of Abuse. This step has two parts. First, sins and iniquities are passed on from one generation to another. Each spouse has to assume responsibility for what they are bringing from their heritage into the marriage. Blood runs thick, so it is best if spouses not criticize each other's families, while being honest about their own. Second, couples have sinned together, and that is best resolved by mutual agreement and confession.

Step Three: Balance Rights and Responsibilities. In troubled marriages spouses attack the character of each other while looking out for their own needs. Both must be responsible for their own character and seek to meet the needs of each other. In what ways haven't they loved, accepted, respected, submitted to, or appreciated each other? In what ways have they tried to control the other, and in what ways haven't they trusted God to convict the other spouse so that he or she can be filled with the Spirit and have self-control?

Step Four: Break Sexual Bondage. We never have the right to violate our spouse's conscience, and we cannot use the body of another to satisfy our lust. Good sex does not make a good marriage, but a good marriage will have righteous sex.

Step Five: Release Old Hurts. Forgiveness is the glue that holds a marriage together.

Step Six: Unmask Satan's Deceptions. Christian marriages are under siege, and it is critical that couples know how to recognize his strategies and know how to stand firm in their faith.

Step Seven: Renew the Marriage. This is a powerful step of committing the couple's marriage, home, and family to the Lord. The process concludes by holding each other's hands and saying their vows. However, instead of saying. "I take you to be . . . ," they say, "I give myself to you to be your wedded husband/wife. . . ."

I would never ask someone to do anything that I wasn't willing to do myself, and neither would Chuck. So we prayed for each other as we went through the process with our wives. We both set a day aside, and we both had an encounter with God and our wives. After thirty-plus years of marriage, there were some issues that we had swept under the carpet, and God has a loving way of pulling the carpet out from under us. Thank you, Jesus. It is amazing how we can let little issues fester by falsely believing that it would be better for the relationship to ignore them than to seek resolution. After the first printing of the book I invited some Christian leaders to a Setting Your Marriage Free weekend retreat. At the completion of the retreat I asked for feedback. Here is what some of them wrote:

> The ineffectiveness of most churches is due to the ineffectiveness of marriages. I have tried all kinds of counseling, but the process in Setting Your Marriage Free deals directly with the source of the conflict and brought life-changing transformation.

> God used this process to resolve all known strongholds that bound us. We are experiencing purification and holiness in all areas of our marriage.

> Yes, it was difficult. Through honest and vulnerable discussion, the Lord led us through problems, anguish, hurts, and fears, all the way to forgiveness, resolution, love, and commitment.

> It opened my eyes to the spiritual forces that would destroy our marriage and gave us the tools to win.

I have been to marriage seminars, attended your conference, and read books on marriage, but this broke the strongholds in our marriage and allowed us to continue in ministry.

This cuts through the "religion" of society and puts us back on Christ's team, in the Word, focused on Him, and entering His work.

This was my last resort, and I was apprehensive. But this real, honest, heartfelt, truthful, godly way softened my heart and gave me back my hope and a desire to truly love my husband.

The Lord got to the heart of our dysfunction. Most of our work on our marriage had been 90 percent psychological and 10 percent spiritual. This was 100 percent spiritual without ignoring the psychological.

Freedom is found in Christ individually first—then as a couple. This method and material got us beyond the surface into the cancer and then finally free.

This process gets to the heart of the issues, provides a format for dealing with them, and brings the truth of God's Word coupled with God's strength to resolve them.

This was a powerful and meaningful experience for us. The Lord performed a significant work in our marriage. This gave us a clean slate. After twenty years we wanted a fresh start, and we got it.

Growing Through Committed Relationships

God works primarily in our lives through committed relationships for two reasons. First, marriage is a covenant relationship and was intended to last until one spouse physically dies. It is not a contract that one can rip up if the other defaults. Homes are like pressure cookers. We either get well done or we blow the top off. There will be trials and tribulations when we live together in the confinement of our homes.

> Therefore, as God's chosen people, holy and dearly loved, clothe yourselves with compassion, kindness, humility, gentleness and patience. Bear with each other and forgive whatever grievances you may have against one another. Forgive as the Lord forgave you. And over all these virtues put on love, which binds them all together in perfect unity.
>
> Galatians 3:12–14 NIV 1984

We should stay true to our commitments, honor our obligations, remain faithful to our vows, and grow up. Where better are we going to learn to love, accept, and forgive one another? If we don't learn it there, where will we? I stumbled across the following years ago:

Marriage License: A Learner's Permit

It's a wise groom who has to be dragged to the altar. He knows what love is. It's death! If the lovers don't know this, they're headed for trouble. Never will you have your way again. You can't be happy if the other person isn't. No matter who wins the argument, you lose. Always. The sooner you learn this, the better off you'll be.

Love is an exercise in frustration. You leave the window up when you want it down. You watch someone else's favorite television program. You kiss when you have a headache. You turn the music down when you like it loud. You learn to be patient without sighing or sulking.

Love is doing things for the other person. In marriage two become one. But the one isn't you. It's the other person. You love this person more than you love yourself. This means that you love this person as he or she is. We should ask ourselves frankly what that impulse is that makes us want to redesign the other person. It isn't love. We want the other person to be normal, like us! But is that loving the other person or ourselves?

Love brings out the best in people. They can be themselves without artificiality. People who know they're loved glow with beauty and charm. Let this person talk. Create the assurance that any idea, any suggestion, any feeling can be expressed and will be respected. Allow the other person to star once in a while. A wife's joke doesn't have to be topped. Don't correct your husband in the middle of his story. Cultivate kind ways of speaking. It can be as simple as asking them instead of telling them what to do.

Don't take yourself too seriously. Married life is full of crazy mirrors to see ourselves. How stubborn, how immature we really are. You may be waiting for your wife to finish because you never lifted a finger to help her.

Love is funny. Its growth doesn't depend on what someone does for you. It's in proportion to what you do for him or her. The country is swarming with people who have never learned this. So are divorce courts.[1]

There is a second reason why God works primarily in our lives to develop Christian character through committed relationships. We can put on a public face for our neighbors, co-workers, and casual friends, but we can't be a phony at home. Our children and spouses will see right through us. When we keep something from our spouses, they may not know what is wrong, but they definitely know something is wrong.

A denominational executive asked me out for lunch and said, "I have heard you say that we can't be our wives' counselor or pastor, and I agree with that. In many ways my wife has been a very good spouse and mother, and she serves God by being the administrator in the church we attend. However, my wife needs some help, and she is open to it, but I also know that I am not the one to give it to her. Would you be willing to meet with her?"

In our first meeting she shared her story, which didn't include any major abuses or conflicts. In fact, she said that she was raised in a good Christian home and was introduced to God at a very early age. She had what she thought was a good marriage and two fine children. She was a well-groomed, articulate woman who exemplified Christian professionalism. There was nothing in her story that would precipitate the personal struggles she was presently having. We agreed to meet the next week and go through the Steps to Freedom in Christ. After we had finished the process, she paused at the door on the way out and said, "It wasn't a good family that I was raised in, was it?" A month later I received the following letter:

> How can I say thanks? The Lord allowed me to spend time with you just when I was concluding that there was no hope for me to ever break free from the downward spiral of continual defeat, depression, and guilt.
>
> Having literally grown up in church and being a pastor's wife for twenty-three years, everyone thought I was as put together on the inside as I was on the outside. On the contrary, I knew that there was no infrastructure on the inside, and often wondered when the weight of trying to hold myself together would cause my life to fall apart and come crumbling down. It seemed as if sheer determination was the only thing that kept me going.
>
> When I left your office last Thursday, it was a beautiful, crystal-clear day with the snow visible on the mountains, and it felt like a film had been lifted from my eyes. The radio was playing an arrangement of "It Is Well With My Soul." The words of the song fairly exploded in my mind with the realization that it was well in my soul for the first time in years.
>
> The next day in the office my immediate response to "How are you today?" was, "I'm doing great! How about you?" In

the past I would have mumbled something about being almost alive. The next comment I heard was, "Boy, something must have happened to you yesterday."

I have heard the same songs and read the same Bible verses as before, but it is as if I'm really hearing them for the first time. There is an underlying joy and peace in the midst of the same circumstances that used to bring defeat and discouragement. For the first time I have wanted to read my Bible and pray. It is hard to contain myself—I want to shout from the rooftop what has taken place in my life.

Already the deceiver has tried to plant thoughts in my mind and tell me that this won't last, that it is just another gimmick that won't work. The difference is that now I know those are lies from Satan and not the truth. What a difference freedom in Christ makes!

How do you think that changed the dynamics of their marriage and the environment at her work? From a broad perspective, biblical history moves from creation and freedom to the fall; from the fall to redemption; from redemption to repentance and faith; and from repentance and faith to freedom. "It was for freedom that Christ set us free" (Galatians 5:1), but you won't experience that freedom if you don't know or believe the truth and haven't repented. From a narrower perspective, Paul's message brings us from spiritual death to life in Christ, followed by instructions to put off the old self (who we were in Adam) and put on the new self (who we are in Christ). Then Paul brings up the subjects of marriage, family, and slavery. Being a slave in those days was very different from the forced submission of modern-day slavery. Slaves were more like employees, and their physical needs were better met by serving their masters than trying to make a living on their own. It was usually a lifetime assignment, and therefore a committed relationship like marriage.

Knowing who we are is the foundation for how we live. The barriers that separated us because of our natural heritage no longer exist: "Here there is no Greek or Jew, circumcised or uncircumcised, barbarian, Scythian, slave or free, but Christ is all, and is in all" (Colossians 3:11 NIV1984). In other words, "in Christ" there are no racial, religious, cultural, or social distinctions; Galatians 3:28 adds neither "male nor female; for you are all one in Christ Jesus."

However, becoming a new creation in Christ does not eradicate social roles, gender, or lines of authority. For instance, in Colossians 3:11 Paul says there is no slave, and then he refers to slaves in Colossians 3:22. Verse 11 is referring to the identity of every child of God, and verse 22 is referring to the social situation in which someone may be called to live. Saying there is neither male nor female did not change the roles of husband and wife, nor did it change our gender. Christian fathers, mothers, children, and employees should live like children of God. Their identity in Christ is the same, and they carry equal status in the kingdom of God, but their roles in society are different. Remember, it isn't what we do that determines who we are. It is who we are that determines what we do.

Polygamy has been a global problem since creation, but the public acceptance of same-sex marriages hasn't been an issue until recently. In these latter days we are experiencing an all-out frontal attack on the sanctity of marriage. Theologically liberal churches and denominations are caving in to social pressure like never before in church history, and it is all happening in the name of love and freedom—but it is neither love nor freedom.

Freedom is not license to do whatever the flesh desires, and freedom does not just lie in the exercise of choice. Freedom is always related to the consequences of the choices we make. People may believe they have the freedom to tell a lie, but they would have to remember whom they told the lie to and what the lie was. They would also have to live with the consequences of telling the lie, which may lead to a loss of trust and severed relationships. Exercising the "freedom of choice" to lie to a spouse can never end well. Christians are free to become all that God intended them to be. They are free from the attachments of the world, the flesh, and the devil.

The world's definition of love (*eros* and *phileo*) is very different from the love (*agape*) of God. *Eros* is erotic or sensual love, which is self-satisfying pleasure. *Phileo* is brotherly love. Jesus said, "If you love those who love you, what credit is that to you? For even sinners love those who love them" (Luke 6:32). *Phileo* is conditional love. God's love is unconditional because it is not dependent upon the object of one's love. God loves us because God is love (see 1 John 4:8). It is His nature to love us. When *agape* is used as a noun, it refers to the character of God.

> Love is patient, love is kind and is not jealous; love does not brag and is not arrogant, does not act unbecomingly; it does not seek its own, is not provoked, does not take into account a wrong suffered, does not rejoice in unrighteousness, but rejoices with the truth; bears all things, believes all things, hopes all things, endures all things. Love never fails.
>
> 1 Corinthians 13:4–8

If we all loved like that, what kind of marriages would we have?

When freedom and love are disjoined from the character of God, they become license and selfishness. "But the goal of our instruction is love from a pure heart and a good conscience and a sincere faith" (1 Timothy 1:5). "For you were called to freedom, brethren; only do not turn your freedom into an opportunity for the flesh, but through love serve one another" (Galatians 5:13). We may not be able to change what the world does, but the world cannot keep us from having a loving relationship with our spouses.

> For this is the will of God, your sanctification; that is, that you abstain from sexual immorality; that each of you know how to possess* his own vessel in sanctification and honor, not in lustful passion, like the gentiles who do not know God.
>
> 1 Thessalonians 4:3–4

---

* The word for *possess* in this passage means "to acquire." It is found in the Septuagint and other literature written at the time of Christ and refers to marrying a wife. The word for *vessel* is never used anywhere else in the Bible to mean "body." It is translated as "wife" in 1 Peter 3:7. The Hebrew equivalent (*keli*) of *vessel* means "wife" in rabbinical writings.

ELEVEN
Setting Your Church Free

One day in Portiuncula while at prayer alone in his cell, St. Francis saw a vision of the whole house surrounded and besieged by devils. They were like a great army surrounding the place, but none of them could gain entrance to the house. The brothers were so disciplined and devoted in their lives of sanctity that the devils were frustrated without a host upon whom they might find a way in.

It happened, in the days soon after Francis's vision, that one of the brothers became offended by another and he began to think in his heart of ways to revenge the slight. While the scheming brother was devising vengeful plans, entertaining wicked thoughts, the devil, finding an open door, entered Portiuncula upon his back.

Francis, the watchful shepherd of his flock, saw that the wolf had entered, intending to devour his little sheep. At once, Francis called the brother to him and asked him to disclose the hatred that had caused this disturbance in his house. The brother, frightened that Francis knew the content of his heart, disclosed to him all of the venom and malice that consumed him, acknowledging his fault and begging humbly for forgiveness.

Loving his sheep as does the Father, the shepherd soon absolved the brother, and immediately, at that moment, before his very face, Francis saw the devil flee from his presence.

The brother returned to the flock and the wolf was gone from the house.[1]

Eight centuries later, Pastor Mark, a gifted evangelist, led many people to Christ in a nominally Christian fellowship. Opposition to Mark's message and leadership style began to surface, and the inevitable struggle for power resulted in a church split. Taking with him the conservative core, Mark started Community Bible Church, which he pastored for ten years. Tragically, he had a moral failure, which led to a bitter departure.

Mark's successor was a young man named Jerry, who was attempting to pastor his first church. He didn't last long. In guarded language, the calling committee at Community Bible Church admitted they had run him off. Jerry probably made a lot of mistakes that inevitably accompany most pastors' first ministry experience. When Community Bible Church extended a call for yet another pastor, John accepted with the understanding that the primary culprits of the original problems were no longer players in the church.

It was a good experience at first, but within months the honeymoon was over. Resistance to John's leadership was increasing at every board meeting. Gossip was rampant, and rumors were floating around the church. He was spending most of his time putting out fires instead of leading in a responsible way. A spiritual pall hung over the church like a brooding vulture. Worship was an arduous task instead of a joyful celebration. The responses to his messages were neutral at best, and there were few visible signs of anybody bearing fruit.

In the past John would have doubled his efforts, but somehow he knew that was not the answer for him or for Community

Bible Church. He sought help for himself, and found his own freedom in Christ. In the past his identity was wrapped up in his role as a pastor, which was being threatened.

Having a new sense of security in Christ, John wanted to help others resolve their conflicts and be established alive and free in Christ. So he began preaching from the book of Ephesians, teaching his people who they are in Christ and helping them realize that their "struggle is not against flesh and blood, but against the rulers, against the authorities, against the powers of this dark world and against the spiritual forces of evil in the heavenly realms" (Ephesians 6:12). At the same time, he began to pore through the minutes of previous board and church meetings. He discovered that the church had not dealt fairly with their previous pastors, nor had they dealt adequately with other moral issues.

John shared his observations with the present board. Although the original leaders were no longer in the church, the same pathology seemed to continue, which is almost always the case. Getting rid of a pastor or ungodly lay leaders doesn't solve the problem by itself. A host of unresolved issues and pain are left in the wake of departing dysfunctional leaders. Being a small church, the board decided to bring the matter before the whole body. A lot of painful memories came to the surface, and it was obvious to everyone that past issues had only been covered up and not adequately dealt with. The church sensed some release after acknowledging their sins and seeking forgiveness from one another.

Pastor John sensed that more needed to be done. So he encouraged the board to contact Jerry, the previous pastor, and ask him if he would be willing to come back to the church for a special service of reconciliation. Jerry was still hurting from the devastating experience and had not returned to the ministry. He declined at first, but finally agreed to come back for the good of both his family and the church he was asked to leave.

As Jerry stood before the church body, the board read a list of offenses the church had committed against him and asked for his forgiveness. They waited as he considered the choice. Finally Jerry responded, "Jesus requires that we forgive others as He has forgiven us. So I choose to forgive you for what you have done to me and my family, and I want to acknowledge the mistakes I made as well." There wasn't a dry eye in the house.

Mark, the founding pastor, refused their invitation, but the board had done all they could to resolve their issues and bring their church into a right relationship with God. Jerry has since returned to ministry. The spiritual pall left the church, and the congregation sensed new life in Christ.

Community Bible Church, Mark, Jerry, and John are fictional names, but the story isn't. As I have traveled across America and around the world, I have had the privilege of talking to many denominational leaders and missionary executives. Based on their observations, about 15 percent of our churches are functioning like living organisms and substantially bearing fruit. Many are spiritually dead and bearing no fruit at all. In the United States there are 1,600 forced resignations by pastors every month. Many of these pastors make up the 1,500 that are leaving the ministry every month due to interpersonal conflict, burnout, and moral failure. Many denominational leaders are overwhelmed with church conflicts. They find themselves like Pastor John, spending most of their time trying to put out fires instead of offering visionary leadership. Many denominational leaders and church consultants are aware that stagnant churches must come to terms with their past, or there is no future.

How can churches repent and resolve their conflicts on a corporate level? That is the subject of my book *Setting Your Church Free*, which I co-wrote with Charles Mylander. Since the first printing we have led many churches, missionary agencies, and parachurch ministries through the process of corporate conflict resolution. The organizations that have submitted to this process have mostly been good churches or ministries that want to get better. One would think that the most dysfunctional churches would jump on the prospect, but they are usually dysfunctional because of the leadership—whether lay leadership, pastoral leadership, or both. Dysfunctional leaders read the book, but they won't submit to the process unless they are willing to humble themselves and seek resolution for their own personal and spiritual conflicts.

Dysfunctional marriages and churches have one issue in common, which you will likely spot in the following diagram on church disciplines. We are not lacking resources that teach how to lead, evangelize, disciple others, and worship. The problem is subtle, because the programs and strategies can still be biblical. Life begins to slip away, however, when confidence and dependence upon God shift to confidence and dependence upon programs and strategies. Searching for a better program or trying to duplicate what other "successful" churches or pastors are doing will not bring new life to the church.

Few churches have contributed more to church growth than First Baptist Church of Modesto, California, did in the eighties and nineties. Thousands from all over the world flocked to their Institute of Church Imperatives. I attended twice when I was a pastor. I also got the chairman of our church board to go and see how a church should function according to the New Testament principles of evangelism and discipleship. It became a model church for some consulting groups who taught First Baptist's principles to other churches. As a seminary professor, I offered credit to students who attended the conference. Tremendous church growth took place, and most of it by conversion. Few churches had as many good spokes in their church disciplines wheel as this church did. Almost all of their staff was homegrown.

After several years of growth, the ministry reached a plateau. Their dynamic pastor, Bill Yaeger, retired, and Wade Estes was handed the mantle. I had the privilege of conducting a conference in this fine church, and while there I shared with them the above diagram. Here is Wade's story in his own words:

> Pastor Bill Yaeger is a man for whom I have great affection. In a very real sense he has been a father in ministry to me, much as Paul was to Timothy. I cannot imagine having a finer or greater ministry legacy than that which I have received from him.
>
> During the 1970s when Bill and the pastoral staff were putting their ministry plan together, the church in America was struggling to understand its mission and its methods to get the gospel out. In 1972, First Baptist Church in Modesto undertook a survey of churches around the country and found that small-group discipleship was almost unheard of. Laymen did not know how to express their faith. Campus Crusade for Christ and Evangelism Explosion took the lead and came through with some great tools. As Bill told me, "There was much to be done just in the basics of 'how do we fly this thing?'" That was the challenge of the day.

The Lord led in a powerful way, as revival broke out. Hundreds of people came to Christ and became a part of small-group Bible studies. In the twenty-four years that Bill was senior pastor, the church grew tenfold. In the early 1970s a vision for training men and women for professional ministry was born. Today, the pastoral staff is almost entirely a second-generation team, trained in our church. More than two hundred men and women from our internship training ministry have been sent out over the past twenty-four years.

The ministry skill training that was imparted to our young pastoral staff (while they were involved in our internship program) was superb in content, modeling, and supervision. However, for many of the younger staff, our confidence slowly came to rest in our ability to duplicate and fine-tune the ministry programs that were entrusted to our leadership.

As with many second-generation ministries, a "program mind-set" (institutionalization) can subtly take over and replace a conscious and intentional dependence upon Christ, without whom we can do nothing (see John 15:5).

Teaching other pastors and leaders through the Institute of Church Imperatives only added to our youthful deception, heightening our sense of self-sufficiency. We would teach the need to seek God's wisdom through prayer, but unconsciously, that was really secondary to hard work and the execution of biblical principles. We slowly became aware that our hard work was no longer bearing the fruit it once had.

A growing sense of discontent began to characterize our staff. We were fine-tuning, tweaking, and renovating every program we had, but the fruit neither increased nor remained (see John 15:16). We were stymied. We began to realize that program motivation was not the answer. But what was? We found ourselves in the same position that Bill was in twenty-four years earlier. We had to seek the Lord's will and leading for the work to which He had called us.

When we finally saw our helplessness, the Lord began revealing the need to fully rely upon Him and not our ability to work for Him. The Lord powerfully led us to spend increasing amounts of time in prayer. We devoted two pastoral staff retreats to prayer and fasting, seeking the Lord's direction and blessing. It became clear that the Lord was calling us to lead the church into a life of dependence upon Him, expressed through prayer.

I preached on prayer for four months in morning worship services. We worked with the leaders of the church to equip them to lead their groups in prayer. I must emphasize that this call to prayer was not a program. It was seeking forgiveness and looking for the blessing and leading of God in our church. It was a resignation to His perfect will, whatever it might be. It was a recognition that without His strength empowering us, without His leading and guiding us, and without the manifestation of His presence in our midst, we were doomed to mediocre ministry.

During this time, a church in our town hosted a Freedom in Christ conference. We sent a few pastoral staff members and some laypeople. They returned with such a glowing report that a few of us began to read *Victory Over the Darkness* and *The Bondage Breaker*. Later, at a pastoral staff retreat, the Lord totally disrupted our schedule following a time of prayer. We shifted gears and viewed a video of a counseling session conducted by Dr. Anderson. I told our staff, "We're not going to just watch this; we need to go through it." As he led the counselee through the Steps to Freedom in Christ, we would listen, turn off the VCR, and go through the Steps ourselves. Later in the week, the Lord led us to contact Freedom in Christ Ministries regarding a conference for our church. We agreed to hold a community-wide conference.

To prepare for the conference, the entire pastoral staff, board of deacons, and other leaders, along with our spouses, blocked out a week and went through the entire conference on video. By the time the conference arrived, about two hundred leaders had worked through the Steps to Freedom in Christ. Two hundred key leaders walking in spiritual freedom is quite an army with which to begin a conference!

On Saturday evening before the event began, Dr. Anderson and I talked about the conference and what the Lord had been doing in our congregation. As we talked, I was overpowered with a renewed assurance that the Lord had been guiding us through the changes we were experiencing. Dr. Anderson explained the trap we had fallen into and the need to be Christ-centered in our ministry as opposed to being program-centered. He made the same presentation to our entire staff later in the week. It crystallized in our hearts and minds the deception we had fallen into and the new path we were on.

When the conference began, the attendance and level of participation were incredible! More than 2,200 people from our church and community were involved. God was working so powerfully in people's lives that we changed our plans for the Sunday morning worship services. We invited people to share with the congregation what God had done in their lives that week. The degree of transparency and love that was openly shared was amazing. It was apparent that people were truly free in Christ!

We are continuing to strive to be a ministry that depends upon Christ and not ourselves or the programs we are able to create and maintain. The patterns of the flesh don't change easily, but we are seeing remarkable progress in our thinking and actions. We still work hard, but we realize that if we only receive the fruit that comes from our hard work, we are missing God's blessing upon our lives and ministry.

I have often wondered if we have emphasized a personal relationship with God at the expense of a corporate relationship with God. In the Old Testament God dealt with nations. In the New Testament Paul's epistles are primarily addressed to churches. That is the case for the seven churches in Revelation 2 and 3, which serves as the model for the Setting Your Church Free process. The goal is to establish Christ as the center of your church, as the following diagram illustrates:

Steps to Setting Your Church Free

I believe the spiritual health of your church can be evaluated on one criteria alone. Is the official board and senior staff of your church a proud group of individuals who are seeking to exert their influence, or are they a group of humble servants united together in Christ seeking God's will? No church can rise above its leadership, and the leaders of a church are responsible for ensuring that God is the functional head of His body. Christian leaders should be like Paul and say, "Follow me as I follow Christ." It should go without saying that all those who participate in the corporate repentance process have already processed the individual Steps to Freedom in Christ.

Read carefully chapters two and three in the book of Revelation. There are about fifty *I*'s in those seven letters to the churches, and *I* is Christ. He is always present, and He knows the thoughts and intentions of everyone's heart. When I help individual inquirers, I do so knowing that they are God's children and that He knows everything about them. That is why God himself is the Wonderful Counselor, and He is also the Wonderful Church Consultant. When I am asked to lead a church through the corporate Steps, I do so knowing that it is His body I am working with and that He knows all their deeds. Each of the seven letters in Revelation ends with the same statement: "He who has an ear, let him hear what the Spirit says to the churches." The question is, *Are we listening?* The next question is, *Do we want God to write our church a letter?*

If your leadership answers yes to those questions, they will hear from God, and by the end of the process they will have a fairly accurate assessment of their church. God doesn't expose our sins and weaknesses to condemn us. He does it so we can repent and return to our first love. We recommend that all the official board members and key pastoral staff be included in the process. Normally we schedule the event for Friday evening and all day Saturday. We recommend that a neutral nonmember facilitate the process, and to have a trustworthy secretary appointed to keep records. The room should be lined with a lot of paper that can be written on. By the end of the day a visible pattern will emerge. The corporate repentance process begins in prayer, just like the individual and marriage Steps do. Every person should be encouraged to share without criticism or condemnation from others. Everyone's perspective is valued.

Step One: Our Strengths. As in the letters in Revelation, we start by asking the Lord to reveal to our minds what we are doing right. Almost every church is doing something well, and it is good to surface that at the beginning, which softens the burden of what comes up later. In this step we try to gain consensus for the five to seven ministries that are working well for the church. We conclude by having the participants stand and say, "We thank God for [name the strengths]." This list is saved for the final Prayer Action Plan.

Step Two: Our Weaknesses. After they have prayed and sat silently before the Lord, the participants are asked to share what they believe are their weaknesses. The recorder will write down everyone's response on the wall. Usually there will be many more weaknesses shared than strengths. We don't try to work for consensus on this step, and we don't try to separate the greatest weaknesses. We just list them for future reference.

Step Three: Memories. Every church has good and painful memories. We start by asking God to reveal to our minds the good memories, and we thank God for them. Asking God to reveal painful memories will end up with a list of names that should be destroyed when the day is done. Keep in mind that each participant should have already forgiven those people who have offended them. Corporate forgiveness is on a different plane. For instance, in Paul's second letter to the church in Corinth, he instructs them to forgive the person they had disciplined:

> But one whom you [plural] forgive anything, I forgive also; for indeed what I have forgiven, if I have forgiven anything, I did it for your sakes in the presence of Christ, so that no advantage would be taken of us by Satan, for we are not ignorant of his schemes.
>
> 2 Corinthians 2:10–11

The church needs to forgive offending persons; otherwise Satan would take advantage of their unforgiveness. Typically there is not a dry eye in the room when this step is done. When we break for lunch, we say, "Is there someone in the room right now that you need to talk to?"

Step Four: Corporate Sins. Individual sins that do not affect the ministry are not included in this process. They should have already been taken care of. Every generation of leaders is responsible for the purity of the church, even if the sins were committed by previous leaders. When Israel and Judah divided, Israel never had one godly king. It was said of every king that he continued in the sins of Jeroboam. I believe anyone of them could have said, "Jeroboam was wrong. We should repent and go back to Jerusalem to worship God." None did, and Israel was no more.

For this step the facilitator should seek discernment from the group, and strive for consensus. This includes sins of omission as well as sins of commission. God may surface corporate sins that happened in the church two or three generations ago. The church I mentioned at the beginning of this chapter was born out of a rebellious split, and the authority of every subsequent pastor was challenged until they confessed it.

Step Five: Spiritual Attacks. Satan will take advantage of churches that refuse to forgive and haven't repented of their corporate sins. If you were the devil and wanted to keep the kingdom of God from advancing, what would you do? I know what I would do, because I think I know what he is doing. First, I would try to divide the minds of believers, because a double-minded person is unstable in all their ways. Second, I would try to divide Christian marriages, because a house divided against itself cannot stand. Third, I would try to divide the church, because united we stand, but divided we fall. The Lord is praying that we be single-minded, that our marriages be one in Christ, and that the church be united as He and the

Father are One. When that doesn't happen, we become like blindfolded warriors who don't know who our enemy is, so we strike out at ourselves and each other. What Jesus sees and what we see are often quite different, as revealed in Revelation:

> [**To Smyrna:**] I know the slander of those who say they are Jews and are not, but are *a synagogue of Satan.* Do not be afraid of what you are about to suffer. I tell you, *the devil* will put some of you in prison to test you, and you will suffer persecution for ten days.
>
> Revelation 2:9–10, emphasis added

What people saw were Jews who slandered the Christians in the Smyrna church. What Jesus saw was a "synagogue of Satan." What people saw were Roman rulers who threw Christians in jail. What Jesus saw was the devil who put some of them in prison. Not all synagogues were demonized, but this one was. Not all authorities believed lies about Christians, but in Smyrna the Roman overlords did. These enemies of the gospel were doing the devil's work, attacking the church in Smyrna.

> [**To Pergamum:**] I know where you live—*where Satan has his throne.* Yet you remain true to my name. You did not renounce your faith in me, even in the days of Antipas, my faithful witness, who was put to death in your city—*where Satan lives.*
>
> Revelation 2:13, emphasis added

What people saw was a city on a hill with major temples in it. What Jesus saw was Satan's throne. What people saw was the center of emperor worship in Asia. What Jesus saw was the city where Satan lived. This place was oppressive to Christians. It killed some of them and threatened the others. This was a dangerous place for a church. The "roaring lion" devoured people in this city (see 1 Peter 5:8). Satan does not headquarter in certain cities today, does he? Or could it be that his strategies have not changed that much?

> [**To Thyatira:**] Now I say to the rest of you in Thyatira, to you who do not hold to her teaching and have not learned *Satan's so-called deep secrets* (I will not impose any other burden on you): Only hold on to what you have until I come.
>
> Revelation 2:24–25, emphasis added

What people saw was a prophetess who taught that, since grace covered every sin, it was okay to indulge in the pagan temple feasts. What Jesus saw was that Satan's secrets were a deception for indulging in sexual sin and satanic rituals. Jesus said church members were about to be struck dead for their sins if they didn't repent (see Revelation 2:21–23).

> [**To Philadelphia:**] I will make those who are of *the synagogue of Satan*, who claim to be Jews though they are not, but are liars—I will make them come and fall down at your feet and acknowledge that I have loved you.
>
> Revelation 3:9, emphasis added

What people saw were two religious groups who had different interpretations about their beliefs. What Jesus saw was a demonized synagogue. What people saw was deep animosity that had religious roots. What Jesus saw was a pack of liars who were about to be proved wrong. What people saw were allegations of the dangerous practices and beliefs of Christians. What Jesus saw was a church wrongly accused. What Jesus saw was a faithful band of people to whom He was about to prove His love, even to their deceived enemies.

I believe that churches are under siege today, but it may not always be for something they are doing wrong. It may be because they are doing something right. It is no sin to be under attack, but sin is inevitable if we don't put on the armor of God and dedicate ourselves, our property, and our ministries to the Lord.

Step Six: Prayer Action Plan. By now the room is filled with sheets of paper. The next step is to synthesize all the lists into a Prayer Action Plan. Look for recurring patterns that have surfaced in the steps on weaknesses, memories, corporate sins, and attacks. Make four columns with these headings:

We Renounce: "We renounce" is our response to Jesus, who requires us to repent.

We Announce: "We announce" is our response to Jesus, who charges us to remember.

We Affirm: "We affirm" is our response to Jesus, who encourages us to hold on.

We Will: "We will" is our response to Jesus, who requires us to obey.

The following is an example of a complete Prayer Action Plan:

Our Greatest Strengths

1. We have a strong unity in Christ that creates a close family feeling and loving relationships.
2. We preach the truth and desire to live it out in holiness and righteousness.
3. We pursue unity, humility, and the Holy Spirit's direction.
4. We have leadership with a servant's heart.
5. We encourage personal participation in Christ.
6. We have a strong and active children's ministry.
7. We have a Christ-led vision for health, growth reproduction, and optimism.

OUR PRAYER ACTION PLAN

WE RENOUNCE

1. We renounce acting independently of God.
2. We renounce acting independently of one another.
3. We renounce our lack of commitment to and practice of spiritual disciplines.
4. We renounce our self-focus that produces apathy to the lost.
5. We renounce inappropriate dependence on the pastor that excuses us from our God-given ministries.
6. We renounce sexual immorality in all its forms.

WE ANNOUNCE

1. We announce that in Christ we have God and all His resources.
2. We announce that in Christ we have mutual dependence on and submission to one another.
3. We announce that in Christ we have continual opportunity to commune with God.
4. We announce that in Christ alone we have the freedom and power to love the unsaved as ourselves.
5. We announce that in Christ we are each equipped for the ministries to which He calls us.
6. We announce that in Christ we have freedom from the power of sin.

WE AFFIRM

1. We affirm that we can do all things through Christ who strengthens us.
2. We affirm that we are united as one body in Christ.
3. We affirm that Christ is knocking at our heart's door, longing for spiritual intimacy with us.
4. We affirm that Christ so loved the lost that He died for their sins to bring them to God.
5. We affirm that it's a high privilege and honor to serve the living God.
6. We affirm that there is no sin that is worth breaking our communion with Christ.

WE WILL

1. We will be diligent in prayer, seeking to obey the will of God.
2. We will be sensitive to one another and yield our rights to one another, seeking the Lord's best for the body.
3. We will renew our commitment to the spiritual disciplines by cutting out or giving up less important things in order to practice them.
4. We will set aside our fear and inconvenience to prayerfully and actively share the love of Christ.
5. We will make ourselves available to exercise our gifts, strengths, and abilities as the Holy Spirit leads us.
6. We will hold each other accountable and pray for one another's purity.

Step Seven: Leadership Strategy. The event ends by having all participants recite the Prayer Action Plan, and they are encouraged to pray through it daily for forty days. It should again be recited every time the staff and board meet for the next year. It is just a shot across the bow if the ship doesn't change its course. So it needs to be implemented in the church and change how the leaders do ministry. The congregation has not gone through the repentant process that the board and staff have. However, they will likely sense that something significant has happened. Many churches have held a church meeting and reported what they have heard from God, and how they plan to implement it. Many have found it necessary to confess to the congregation leadership sins of commission and omission. Some pastors will preach a series of messages that address the issues that were raised during the process. Some may come to the weekend with apprehension, but they don't leave that way. The following is an interim pastor's report:

> I purchased a set of Neil's CDs on Resolving Personal and Spiritual Conflicts. After listening to them I began applying his principles to my problems. I realized that some of my problems could be spiritual attacks, and I learned how to take a stand and won victories over some of my problems in my life.
>
> But that was only a tip of the iceberg. I'm a deacon and preacher in a Baptist church. My pastor was suffering from depression and other problems that I was not aware of, and he committed suicide. This literally brought our church to its knees. I knew of some of the problems of the previous pastors and felt it was spiritual, but I didn't know how to relay it to the people, since the devil or a demon cannot affect a Christian. *Right.*
>
> The church elected me as their interim pastor. While in a local bookstore I saw a book of yours, *Setting Your Church Free.* I purchased and read it. I felt with all the spiritual suppression in our church this was the answer. There was only one

problem—how to get the rest of the church to believe. After a few weeks of preaching on spiritual issues, I knew we had to do what you instructed in *Setting Your Church Free*. The previous pastor who killed himself would not believe your material; he would never read or listen to your message.

Slowly, very slowly, the people accepted my messages, and I was able to contact one of your staff. He flew to Houston and led the leaders of our church through the Steps to Setting Your Church Free. The leaders loved it. I felt step one was past. Next I wanted to take all the people through the Steps to Freedom in Christ. Six weeks later, I was able to do so. I really don't understand it, but we were set free from the spiritual bondage of multiple problems. Can't put it all in a letter, or I would write a book.

During all of this, one of our middle-aged members, who was an evangelist, was set free. He learned who he is in Christ and is back in ministry—praise the Lord. I saw the daughters of the deceased pastor set free and able to forgive their father, and they were able to go on with their lives. At one point, one of the girls was contemplating suicide.

This is a new church; God is free to work here! In September we founded our pulpit committee. Our church voted 100 percent for our new pastor. This has never happened in our church before, and this is an independent and fundamental Baptist church. Well, when you do things God's way, you get God's results.

I also work one night a week in our county jail, which is the second largest in the country. I work with the homosexual men, and I have seen many set free.

That is how you become a disciple-making church.

Appendix

How FICM Can Help You
Grow a Disciple-Making Church

Having read this book, what is your conclusion about your own church? Are you a disciple-making church? Freedom in Christ Ministries believes in the church! Our passion is to help church leaders make fruitful, growing disciples who are making a real impact for Christ in their communities. If you are a church leader anywhere in the world, please consider us a resource freely available to you.

Our strategy is straightforward. We create Christ-centered and biblically based resources, and we back them up with training for you and other leaders in your church. Internationally, our main discipleship resource is the award-winning Freedom in Christ discipleship course. It's a proven and effective way for churches to help Christians become established alive and free in Christ through genuine repentance and faith in God. It's been used all over the world and is now available in several languages. Here is what some leaders have to say about it:

I have seen people's understanding revolutionized, their whole approach to the Christian journey transformed. The course has had a dramatic effect on the life of the church. There is a huge new wave of love, compassion, and encouragement among us. Some tired old mind-sets have been released and renewed, and there have been huge leaps in understanding in those who were open to taking God at His word and running with it. There is a VIBRANT buzz of expectation of Jesus' healing and restoration. I am so excited about what Jesus has done through the course.

One of the strengths of Freedom in Christ materials is that they are based on the fundamental fact that most Christians' behavioral problems are, at root, belief problems. As the truth is brought to individuals and they believe it, they become free.

We consider the Freedom in Christ course to be the best material on the market to build Christians up in their walk with Jesus. It encourages personal responsibility and helps people to go deeper with God and discover His blessings. The impact on our church and community has been enormous.

To get connected with Freedom in Christ Ministries in your country, please go to www.ficminternational.org, where you will find details of the contact in your country and an explanation of what resources and equipping are available. Rich Miller, president of FICM-USA, has outlined below how our U.S. office equips American churches.

Steve Goss, executive director,
Freedom in Christ Ministries-International, Reading, England

Becoming a Disciple-Making Church in the United States

The mandate from Jesus Christ to go and make disciples is clear. But how does that happen? How can we remove the obstacles that are in the way of God's people becoming growing, fruitful disciples (see Isaiah 57:14)? That's what this book has been all about. In this brief appendix we will introduce you to a strategy that a growing number of churches in the United States are implementing for the purpose of growing fruitful disciples. We call it the Community Freedom Ministry strategy. What is a Community Freedom Ministry?

A Community Freedom Ministry (CFM) is a teaching environment of grace and truth started by an individual, couple, or group of individuals under church authority who are seeking to establish a "freedom presence" in a locale.

That "freedom presence" involves *teaching* the message of freedom as described in the chapters of this book; *taking* people through a process of resolving personal and spiritual conflicts, called the Steps to Freedom in Christ; and *training* people to take other individuals through the Steps. It is a strategy to bridge the gap between *salvation* and *maturity* in Christ. It is a strategy of making disciples who are growing and bearing fruit under the authority and supervision of a local church's leadership (with FICM providing resources, encouragement, and a supportive prayer network).

Typically, conservative churches do a good job of presenting the plan of salvation, urging people to come to faith in Jesus. That is a great start, but what then? How do converts become growing, fruitful disciples of Jesus? How do we facilitate an environment that is a "spiritual greenhouse" in our churches, conducive for people to experience real growth in Christ?

Simply encouraging those folks to be faithful in church attendance or even plugging them in to a class or small group where good biblical curriculum is offered isn't going to be enough to produce mature believers. In these days of moral decline and family disintegration in America, people are dragging a whole boatload of baggage into their Christian faith. They need to know the truth about their identity, position, and authority in Christ so that they can walk in submission to God and true freedom by overcoming the world, the flesh, and the devil. They need a discipleship strategy that gives them a fighting chance to release their baggage and be set free from their bondage so that they can become growing, fruitful disciples. In short, they need a place to get *unstuck*. The writer of Hebrews put it this way:

> Therefore, since we have so great a cloud of witnesses surrounding us, let us also lay aside every encumbrance and the sin that so easily entangles us, and let us run with endurance the race that is set before us, fixing our eyes on Jesus, the author and perfecter of faith.
>
> Hebrews 12:1–2

When such a strategy is undergirded by a fervent movement of prayer, all heaven can break loose in a church. People who have been "stuck" are finally able to gain spiritual traction and can begin to seek and serve God in meaningful and powerful ways. In other words, they start living as growing, fruitful disciples of Jesus.

Perhaps the best way to introduce you to the CFM strategy and how it can work in a church is by telling the story of a pastor and the church he leads and how this message and ministry have impacted both. After you hear how the Lord has touched and is using this pastor, we'll fill in some of the blanks and hopefully give you a clearer picture of ways you can connect with FICM-USA. We would love to serve you and your church, if the Lord so directs.

I first met Keith when he was a youth pastor. He had invited me to teach freedom principles at a youth retreat he was holding. Halfway through the retreat, all the kids and leaders were scheduled to go white-water rafting. Keith was pumped to go, but he badly wrenched his back that morning and had to stay behind. He was not a happy camper.

I happened to be hanging around the retreat site with my wife, Shirley, and our three very small children, enjoying a break from a wearying summer schedule. Then I spotted Keith limping around the grounds. "Hey, Keith!" I yelled. "Since you are here with nothing to do, how about I take you through the Steps to Freedom in Christ?" We don't normally recommend that kind of direct approach, but as it turned out, the Lord was in it.

Keith, being pretty much in agony and bummed out for missing the rafting trip, told me later that inside he was thinking, *That's the last thing I want to do.* But wanting to sound spiritual, he said, "Sure! Why not?"

It took several hours to guide Keith through that process of repentance and faith, but it was well worth the time we invested. Keith's freedom appointment turned out to be life-changing for him as he dealt with some deep abandonment and other painful issues where he needed to make the tough choice to forgive.

Fast-forward twenty years. . . . Keith had been growing in his understanding of freedom in Christ and had become pastor of a two-campus church outside of Minneapolis. He was looking for a biblical approach to discipleship that went beyond *information* and involved real heart and life *transformation*. In 2014 he became aware of the CFM strategy of FICM-USA, checked out our website, www.ficm.org, and decided to enroll twenty-two of his key leaders and their spouses in our online training institute, CFM University. Pastors, elders, prayer leaders, recovery ministry leaders—you name it—all enrolled in the Coordinator Track, which included our two core courses, CFM 101 and CFM 201, and a practicum.

The CFMU Coordinator Track is academically challenging, personally inspiring, and practically effective in equipping and empowering people to build a ministry of growing fruitful disciples. Many times CFMU students are laypeople who are equipped and empowered to genuinely help people in the congregation walk in freedom and begin to grow. It is a great encouragement and relief for pastoral staff, as a significant ministry load can be taken off their shoulders.

CFMU Coordinator Track students thoroughly study *Victory Over the Darkness* and *The Bondage Breaker* and take an online entrance exam based on those books. Then they go through the two online courses that prepare them to develop a discipleship ministry or CFM in their church. Those online courses are followed by the practicum, where they are given hands-on experience with mentors. They learn how to develop a ministry team, how to build a strong prayer movement to undergird their ministry of discipleship, how (as a layperson) they can work effectively with church leaders, how to develop a teaching and training schedule to launch their ministry, and how to prepare in advance for the enemy's opposition to their discipleship ministry.

The twenty-two leaders in Minnesota took about four months to work through the online material in their spare time during evenings and weekends. They finished up just in time for the four-day practicum, which we held at their church. During the practicum, all twenty-two leaders had their own personal freedom appointment of going through the Steps to Freedom in Christ. They actually took one another through the Steps under the supervision of a trained coach from FICM-USA who traveled in for the purpose of equipping them in the use of this discipleship tool. The testimonies of touched lives after these freedom appointments is one of the highlights of the practicum. Because of their freshly renewed freedom, these leaders are now developing strategies to weave this message, method, and ministry into every aspect of church life. They are following Jesus' mandate to "make disciples," and now they have a strategy to accomplish that very thing, by the grace of God.

One week prior to the practicum, the church had buried a twelve-year-old boy who had taken his own life. My heart broke for that family, and I prayed for them all during that week. I prayed that I might get to meet the parents to encourage their hearts. That meeting happened just before I was to preach at the first service on the Sunday after the practicum. The boy's parents attended the service where I was teaching "Our Identity in Christ: The Antidote to Shame." After that service, the parents met with Keith and said to him, "If only we had heard this message three weeks ago; perhaps things would have turned out differently."

Sadly, the battle for one young boy was lost. But this church is already winning other battles of seeing souls saved, lives transformed, and hearts set free to become growing, fruitful disciples.

It is exciting to watch church leaders personally grab hold of this message, and not just in theory but in practice. As their own lives are touched and transformed, the Lord infuses His zeal in their hearts for others to find the freedom to become growing, fruitful disciples. Pastors are always ministering to others, but who ministers to them? They get wounded and worn out and have struggles in life like everyone else. But where do they go for help?

Pastor Keith said:

> I see the whole message and ministry of Freedom in Christ impacting our body. It is permeating every program we have and every message we present. It's speaking life into people. The freedom message influences our worship and our preaching, and

I have seen it impact our youth ministries, children's ministries, and adult ministries. It enables us to constantly speak a message of hope to those in our congregation and to remind them of their identity in Christ. As I pray with people over the phone or in person, I will often encourage them, "Just remember who you are in Christ." I can't say enough good things about what this message and ministry have done to equip us to help our people not only to grapple with their issues but to understand their true identity as children of God.

If you would like to know more about what Freedom in Christ Ministries-USA has to offer pastors and other church leaders, please visit our website, www.ficm.org. There is a Church Leaders section with free resources that you can download and use. Maybe you want to dig in a little deeper to discover what FICM-USA is all about. If that's the case, we have designed a ministry tool, "Growing Fruitful Disciples: An Introduction to the Freedom in Christ Ministries Approach to Discipleship." You can watch our short trailer for "Growing Fruitful Disciples" (GFD) on our website, and if that piques your interest, you can then watch the three video sessions on the message, method, and ministry of Freedom in Christ. Those professionally filmed videos will give you a good picture of who we are and what we do. The sessions are broken up into short scenes so you can watch them in bite-sized chunks or all at once at your leisure from the comforts of home. There is a feedback form online that you can fill out to let us know how we can serve you and your church.

If you are interested in learning about our online training institute, you can also go directly to the CFM University website, www.cfmuniversity.org, and watch a short video introducing CFMU. The university courses are hosted by the Moodle learning management system utilized by many academic institutions' online classes. If you are interested in enrolling in CFMU, you can go directly to www.freedominchrist.com, which is our FICM-USA online store, and click on the link to CFM University. You will see the options for student enrollment on that webpage.

The biblical teachings and tools of Dr. Neil Anderson have touched individuals, families, and churches all over the world. Perhaps the Lord has used the pages of this book to stir your heart. Maybe you are yearning for a fresh touch from the Spirit of God in your life so that you can be free to walk in newness of life *in Christ*. If you have questions or would just like to dialogue with us, please do not hesitate to contact us by email (info@ficm.org) or by phone (865-342-4000). We count it a privilege to serve you.

In Christ's grace and truth,
Rich Miller, president, FICM-USA

Notes

Chapter 1: Victory Over the Darkness

1. Alexander Balmain Bruce, *The Training of the Twelve*, 2nd ed. (New Canaan, CT: Keats Publishing, 1979), 69.

2. John Stott, *Romans: God's Good News for the World* (Downers Grove, IL: InterVarsity Press, 1994), 187.

Chapter 2: Battle for the Mind

1. F. F. Bruce, *Commentary on the Book of Acts* (Grand Rapids, MI: Eerdmans, 1954), 114.

2. Ernst Haenchen, *The Acts of the Apostles* (Philadelphia: Westminster Press, 1971), 237.

3. Martin Luther, *Table Talk*, IV, 5097, cited in Father Louis Coulange [pseud. Joseph Turmell], *The Life of the Devil* (London: Alfred A. Knopf, 1929), 147. The book includes many references of the devil putting thoughts into the minds of noted saints.

Chapter 3: Discipleship Counseling

1. Mark R. McMinn and Timothy R. Philips, eds., *Care for the Soul* (Downers Grove, IL: InterVarsity Press, 2010), 10–11.

2. The first study involved thirty participants who answered a ten-item questionnaire; the second involved fifty-five participants who answered a twelve-item questionnaire; the third involved twenty-one participants who also answered a twelve-item questionnaire before completing the Steps and again three months afterward.

3. This research was conducted by the board of the Ministry of Healing (based in Tyler, Texas), chaired by Dr. George Hurst, former director of the University of Texas at Tyler Health Center. Conference 1 took place in Oklahoma City,

Oklahoma; conference 2 took place in Tyler, Texas, and was completed in cooperation with a doctoral student at Regent University under the supervision of Dr. Fernando Garzon (doctor of psychology).

4. F. L. Garzon et al., "Freedom in Christ: Quasi-Experimental Research on the Neil Anderson Approach," *Journal of Psychology and Theology* 29 (Spring 2001): 41–51. (Published by Rosemeade School of Psychology, Biola University.)

5. Charles Caldwell Ryrie, *The Ryrie Study Bible* (Chicago: Moody Press, 1995), 1,949.

6. *The Orthodox Study Bible* (Nashville: Thomas Nelson, 1993), 519.

Chapter 4: A Strategy for Making Reproducible Disciples

1. Wayne Grudem in Neil Anderson, *Liberating Prayer* (Eugene, OR: Harvest House, 2012), 5.

Chapter 5: Overcoming Anger

1. Alexander Pope, *An Essay on Man*, ep. 2, st. 14, lines 17–20.

Chapter 6: Overcoming Anxiety Disorders

1. Edmund J. Bourne, *The Anxiety and Phobia Workbook*, 2nd. ed. (Oakland, CA: New Harbinger Publications, Inc., 1995).

2. Edmund J. Bourne, *Healing Fear* (Oakland, CA: New Harbinger Publications, Inc., 1998), 2.

3. Ibid., 5.

4. Quoted in Elisabeth Elliot, *Shadow of the Almighty: The Life and Testament of Jim Elliot* (New York: Harper Collins, 1979), 15.

5. David G. Benner, *Baker Encyclopedia of Psychology* (Grand Rapids, MI: Baker Book House, 1990), 786.

6. Carlos G. Valles, *Let Go of Fear* (New York: Triumph Books, 1991), 88.

Chapter 7: Overcoming Depression

1. Anne Olivier Bell and Andrew McNeillie, eds., *The Diary of Virginia Woolf* (New York: Harcourt, Brace, Jovanovich, 1984), 226.

2. Quoted in Michael Burlingame, *The Inner World of Abraham Lincoln* (Urbana: University of Illinois Press, 1994), 100.

3. Ibid, 93.

4. Ibid, 97.

5. Anthony Storr, *Churchill's Black Dog, Kafka's Mice, and Other Phenomena of the Human Mind* (New York: Grove Press, 1988), n.p.

6. Kay Redfield Jamison, *Touched With Fire: Manic-Depressive Illness and the Artistic Temperament* (New York: Free Press Paperbacks, 1993), 268–270.

7. Kay Redfield Jamison, *An Unquiet Mind: A Memoir of Moods and Madness* (New York: Vintage Books, 1995).

8. Michael Lemonick, "The Mood Molecule," *Time*, September 29, 1997, 75.

9. Ibid., 76.

10. Julie Appleby, "Sales Pitch: Drug Firms Use Perks to Push Pills," *USA Today,* May 16, 2011, http://usatoday30.usatoday.com/news/health/2001-05-16 -perks-usat.htm.

11. Associated Press, "Are Patients Getting the Right Drugs?," CBSNews.com, April 29, 2002, http://www.cbsnews.com/news/are-patients-getting-the-right-drugs/.

12. Thomas J. Moore, *Prescription for Disaster: The Hidden Dangers in Your Medicine Cabinet* (New York: Simon & Schuster, 1998), 115.

13. D. A. Kessler, "Introducing MEDWatch," *Journal of the American Medical Association* 269 (1993): 2765–2768.

14. Mitch and Susan Golant, *What to Do When Someone You Love Is Depressed* (New York: Villard Books, 1996), 10.

15. Ibid., 11.

16. Martin Seligman, *Learned Optimism* (New York: Pocket Books, 1990), 65–66.

17. Archibald Hart, *Counseling the Depressed* (Waco, TX: Word, 1987), 99.

18. Daniel Goleman, *Emotional Intelligence: Why It Can Matter More Than IQ,* 10th anniv. ed. (New York: Bantam Dell, 2005), 71.

Chapter 8: Overcoming Sexual Strongholds

1. "Tracking the Hidden Epidemics 2000: Trends in STDs in the United States," Centers for Disease Control and Prevention, accessed October 15, 2015, http:// www.cdc.gov/std/Trends2000/Trends2000.pdf.

2. Dale S. Kuehne, *Sex and the iWorld: Rethinking Relationship Beyond an Age of Individualism* (Grand Rapids, MI: Baker Academic, 2009).

3. The Williams Institute, "Just the Facts: LGBT Data Overview 2015," UCLA School of Law, accessed October 15, 2015, http://www.scribd.com/doc/263796139 /Just-the-Facts-LGBT-Data-Overview-2015.

4. "Answers to Your Questions: For a Better Understanding of Sexual Orientation and Homosexuality," American Psychological Association, accessed October 15, 2015, http://www.apa.org/topics/lgbt/orientation.pdf.

5. Tim Stafford, "The Best Research Yet," *Christianity Today,* October 2007, 52.

6. Stanton Jones and Mark Yarhouse, *Ex-Gays? A Longitudinal Study of Religiously Mediated Change in Sexual Orientation* (Downers Grove, IL: IVP Academic, 2007).

Chapter 10: Setting Marriages Free

1. "Men Are From Mars . . . Part 3, Ephesians 5:23–24," *Countdown! Golden Minutes Ministries Newsletter* (Long Beach, CA), October 1996, quoted at "Marriage License: A Learner's Permit," Bible.org, accessed October 16, 2015, https:// bible.org/illustration/marriage-license-learner's-permit.

Chapter 11: Setting Your Church Free

1. Paul Sabatier, *The Road to Assisi: The Essential Biography of St. Francis* (Brewster, MA: Paraclete Press, 2003), 167.

Books and Resources by Dr. Neil T. Anderson

Core Material

Victory Over the Darkness (Bethany House, 2000) has a study guide, audiobook, and DVD. With over 1,400,000 copies in print, this core book explains who you are in Christ, how to walk by faith in the power of the Holy Spirit, how to be transformed by the renewing of your mind, how to experience emotional freedom, and how to relate to one another in Christ.

The Bondage Breaker (Harvest House, 2000) has a study guide and audiobook. With over 1,400,000 copies in print, this book explains spiritual warfare, what our protection is, ways that we are vulnerable, and how we can live a liberated life in Christ.

Discipleship Counseling (Bethany House, 2003) combines the concepts of discipleship and counseling and teaches the practical integration of theology and psychology for helping Christians resolve their personal and spiritual conflicts through repentance and faith in God.

Steps to Freedom in Christ (Bethany House, 2004) and interactive video is a discipleship counseling tool that helps

Christians resolve their personal and spiritual conflicts through genuine repentance and faith in God.

Restored (E3 Resources) is an expansion of *Steps to Freedom in Christ* with additional explanation and instruction.

Walking in Freedom (Bethany House, 2008) is a twenty-one-day devotional used for follow-up after leading someone through the Steps to Freedom in Christ.

Freedom in Christ Small-Group Bible Study (Bethany House, 2008) is a discipleship course for Sunday school classes and small groups. The course comes with a leader's guide, a student's guide, and a DVD covering twelve lessons and the Steps to Freedom in Christ. This course is designed to enable believers to resolve personal and spiritual conflicts and be established alive and free in Christ.

The Bondage Breaker DVD Experience (Harvest House, 2011) is also a discipleship course for Sunday school classes and small groups. It is similar to the one above, but the lessons are fifteen minutes instead of thirty minutes. It has a student's guide, but no leader's guide.

The Daily Discipler (Bethany House, 2005) is a practical systematic theology. It is a culmination of Dr. Anderson's books covering the major doctrines of the Christian faith and the problems Christians face. It is a five-day-per-week, one-year study that will thoroughly ground believers in their faith.

VICTORY SERIES (Bethany House, 2014, 2015) is a comprehensive curriculum including eight books that follow the growth sequence of being rooted in Christ, growing in Christ, living in Christ, and overcoming in Christ: *God's Story for You, Your New Identity, Your Foundation in Christ, Renewing Your Mind, Growing in Christ, Your Life in Christ, Your Authority in Christ, Your Ultimate Victory.*

Specialized Books

The Bondage Breaker, The Next Step (Harvest House, 2011) has several testimonies of people finding their freedom from all kinds of problems, with commentary by Dr. Anderson. It is an important learning tool for encouragers. The book gives hope to those who are entangled in sin.

Overcoming Addictive Behavior with Mike Quarles (Bethany House, 2003) explores the path to addiction and how a Christian can overcome addictive behaviors.

Overcoming Depression with Joanne Anderson (Bethany House, 2004) explores the nature of depression, which is a body, soul, and spirit problem, and presents a wholistic answer for overcoming this "common cold" of mental illnesses.

Daily in Christ with Joanne Anderson (Harvest House, 2000) is a popular daily devotional being used by thousands of Internet subscribers every day.

Who I Am in Christ (Bethany House, 2001) has thirty-six short chapters describing who believers are in Christ and how their deepest needs are met in Him.

Freedom From Addiction with Mike and Julia Quarles (Bethany House, 1997) begins with Mike and Julia's journey into addiction and codependency, and explains the nature of chemical addictions and how to overcome them in Christ.

One Day at a Time with Mike Quarles (Bethany House, 2000) is a 365-day devotional helping those who struggle with addictive behaviors and explains how to discover the grace of God on a daily basis.

Freedom From Fear with Rich Miller (Harvest House, 1999) explains the nature of fear, anxiety, and panic attacks and how to overcome them.

Setting Your Church Free with Charles Mylander (Bethany House, 2006, 2014) explains servant leadership and how the leadership of a church can resolve corporate conflicts through corporate repentance.

Setting Your Marriage Free with Dr. Charles Mylander (Bethany House, 2006, 2014) explains God's divine plan for marriage and the steps that couples can take to resolve their difficulties.

Christ-Centered Therapy with Dr. Terry and Julie Zuehlke (Zondervan, 2000) explains the practical integration of theology and psychology for professional counselors, and provides them with biblical tools for therapy.

Getting Anger Under Control with Rich Miller (Harvest House, 1999) explains the basis for anger and how to manage our emotions.

Grace That Breaks the Chains with Rich Miller and Paul Travis (Harvest House, 2003, 2014) explains the bondage of legalism and how to overcome it by the grace of God.

Winning the Battle Within (Harvest House, 2008) shares God's standards for sexual conduct, the path to sexual addiction, and how to overcome sexual strongholds.

Restoring Broken Relationships (Bethany House, 2015) explains the primary ministry of the church, and how we can be reconciled to God and each other.

Rough Road to Freedom (Monarch Books, 2012) is Dr. Anderson's memoir.

For more information, contact Freedom in Christ Ministries:

Canada: freedominchrist@sasktel.net or www.ficm.ca

India: isactara@gmail.com

Switzerland: info@freiheitinchristus.ch or www.freiheitin christus.ch

United Kingdom: info@ficm.org.uk or www.ficm.org.uk

FICM-USA: info@ficm.org or www.ficm.org

FICM-International: www.ficminternational.org

Dr. Neil T. Anderson was formerly the chairman of the Practical Theology Department at Talbot School of Theology. In 1989, he founded Freedom in Christ Ministries, which now has staff and offices in various countries around the world. He is currently on the Freedom in Christ Ministries International Board, which oversees this global ministry. For more information about Dr. Anderson and his ministry, visit his website at www.ficminternational.org.

More From
Neil T. Anderson

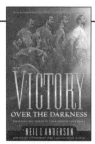
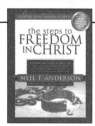
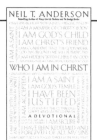